We Never Left You

Beth M Olsen And Richard J Olsen
with Andrea Cagan

ISBN: 151467792X
ISBN 13: 9781514677926
Library of Congress Control Number: 2015910353
CreateSpace Independent Publishing Platform
North Charleston, South Carolina

Table of Contents

Dedication

This book is dedicated to our five children: Jessica, Joshua, Gabriel, Benjamin, and Grace.

Authors' Note

*T*HIS BOOK IS the story of our journey. It is our path, and it has worked for us. It is by no means the only path. It is our hope that you will get out of this book what you need. We have seen the impact that the hope and healing of this story brings and sincerely wish that you will share it with others as we have been able to do.

With love,
Beth and Rick

Foreword

TOWARD THE END of September 2014, I received an intriguing inquiry. A couple, Rick and Beth Olsen, who lived in Glenbeulah, a small Wisconsin town along the Mullet River, sent me this e-mail, written by Beth:

> In 1999, our family was involved in a car accident. A drunk driver ran through a red light and broadsided our minivan. My husband and I survived, but our nine-year-old daughter and seven-year-old son were killed. We have been on quite a journey since then.
>
> As any family would, we struggled with the loss and impact to our lives. We ended up taking a more nontraditional course of healing because the normal paths didn't seem to help. Over the course of the last fifteen years, we have had many experiences to help us understand, including some messages about life after death. By sharing some of these stories with people we know, we have been able to help others to accept and understand loss and death. We have come to realize that we were put in this position to help others. We have often talked about writing a book, but only recently does the energy seem right to get this accomplished.

They had gotten my name from a previous client and I contacted them. We made an immediate connection, and within a couple of weeks, they were on an airplane to Los Angeles to begin a collaboration with me for a book they felt compelled to write. And I felt compelled to help them do it. I had never heard of anyone suffering this severe a tragedy and not only surviving but *thriving*. When I met them, I knew for sure that it was not lip service, and they were not pretending to be more OK or advanced than they were. They were representing themselves accurately. Miraculously, despite what had happened to them, they embodied acceptance, forgiveness, and gratitude.

Shortly after the Olsens arrived at my house, I asked them to describe the tragic accident that took the lives of their two children fifteen years prior. Beth started by saying, "We all piled into the car on a Sunday afternoon to go to the mall. Rick was driving, I was in the passenger seat, and the kids were in the back with their seat belts buckled. We had a minivan because we thought it would be safer for the kids in the event of a head-on collision."

While they painted a picture in meticulous detail of the drunk driver crashing into them at eighty miles an hour, I cried with them. I felt breathless and helpless as I learned exactly how and when each child passed over from this world to the next. How could they sit there, I wondered, and talk about the day their lives were shattered beyond recognition without falling to pieces or becoming rigid, cold, and distant? It was simply a fact that these two warm, loving, seemingly ordinary Midwesterners had never abandoned or blamed each other or themselves for their loss. Even closer than before, they had regained the ability to smile and enjoy life, and they were raising three more children now, all of whom had arrived after the devastation.

I interviewed Rick and Beth for six uninterrupted hours that day. They clearly believed that there was a reason for their loss, that it was meant to happen. They had made peace with themselves and each other, and they were ready and willing to embark on their mission in life—to help other people in similar circumstances. I was stunned by their resilience, strength, faith, and hopefulness. It was not that they believed they could bring their children back or were pretending that they were back;

rather, they believed that there was a way to contact them, to communicate with them in real time, and to remain connected with them forever.

When they left my home for their hotel in the early evening, I felt like I knew their children, Jessica and Joshua, intimately and individually, from her thoughtful sweetness and her love of Winnie the Pooh, to his determination and energetic playfulness. They made me smile, and they were on my mind when I dropped off to sleep that night, imagining them playing together and laughing, which was what they loved to do.

I woke up early the next morning, before six, and had just wandered upstairs to put on the coffee before Rick and Beth arrived for another day of interviews when I heard some unfamiliar bird calls. I live in a canyon with trees, birds, and small animals, but this wasn't the usual cooing from the mourning doves that liked to gather at my outdoor fountain at dawn. It was a deeper sound, one that I didn't recognize.

When I looked through the glass door just off the dining room that leads out to a deck, I gazed upward and saw two large gray owls with white feathered patches on their chests perched on the eaves of my roof, taking turns hooting to one another. I didn't know if they were native to the canyon or not but I stood, mesmerized. The sunrise was just beginning to light up the world behind these magical-looking creatures that I was seeing for the first time, even though I'd lived in my house for more than twenty years. It felt like a visitation, something beyond the mundane, and I remained motionless, stunned at the beauty and majesty of these owls who were singing and bringing in a new day on the edge of my roof.

I listened and watched as they both snapped their heads in my direction at the same time and gazed at me, their huge eyes meeting mine. They went quiet for a few moments and stared directly at me as we silently acknowledged one another's presence. When they turned their heads back and took up their song once again, I slowly walked away and found my iPhone so I could take a picture of them. I needed proof that they were real and not a figment of my imagination.

I managed to snap three photos before one of the owls flew away. When the second one took off in the same direction, I saw Jessica and

Joshua in my mind's eye. I believed they had visited me, called out to me, and let me know they approved; they were in harmony with me, and they wanted me to help their parents tell their story. Most of all, they wanted me to know that they were there—*really there*. I could have missed the sign altogether and walked past them and into the kitchen. But I had stopped and listened. I was convinced that they were watching over me and the creation of this book. I don't know how I knew this. I just did.

When I sat down to have some coffee, I recalled the Olsens telling me that while it took Beth a little longer than Rick to make peace with what had happened, they had come to accept that there was nothing they could have done to change the circumstances around the accident. In fact, they believed that it was supposed to happen; it was part of something that Spirit had in mind for them, and now they had roles to fulfill that required them to look at things in a much broader scope and measure of time.

Today, they are living examples that it is possible to survive extreme loss and find the desire and will to carry on. By writing this book, they have found a way, in the aftermath of every parent's worst nightmare, to reach outside themselves and help others who are suffering from great loss. They believe wholeheartedly that it is possible to create new meaning and purpose in life and not only to survive great loss, but also to make life rich and beautiful once again—because they have done it.

Today, they feel that anyone can follow in their footsteps and maintain a relationship with someone who has died. They may not have the kind of relationship with Joshua and Jessica in the physical sense that they would prefer, but Rick and Beth know that their children are still here and they can pray to them and talk with them, because they are convinced that life goes on. They have received the signs, and they have responded with open hearts. While the signs that come to each individual may be different from Rick's and Beth's, they serve the same purpose—to show the living that the dead are not gone and there is a way to connect and communicate with them.

In the pages that follow, the Olsens describe the accident that changed their lives forever, including the aftermath, the funeral, the sentencing, the obvious signposts that led them to their children, and the people who influenced them as they struggled to create new meaning in their day-to-day lives after a great tragedy. They take their readers on a roller-coaster ride from normal life to sudden shock, from grief to acceptance, and from darkness to light. Rick and Beth have found a way to carry on. They want us all to know, not because they are more special or advanced than anyone else, but rather because they are the same as anyone else. The only difference is that due to circumstances beyond their control, they discovered that life after death is real and available, whether anyone else believes it or not.

As they shine a beacon of light to those who are stumbling along in the terrible void that follows tragedy and sudden death, they are demonstrating that there is a way out. They have found it, and they are ready and willing to pass it on to anyone who is courageous enough to believe that with death, all is not lost. They agree that a new relationship with those who have passed and a new way of connecting can begin with a little faith, a lot of hope, and a strong desire to accept and be nourished by things that we cannot necessarily explain or understand.

"Find your inner knowing and trust it," Beth says. "It will show you the way."

"Stay open to possibility," Rick adds, "and the spirit world will conspire on your behalf for your good. All you have to do is ask."

—Andrea Cagan

Olsen family 1997

1

American Girl

Beth

FOR THE LAST fifteen years, I've been waiting for a text from God. I'm happy these days. My life is great, and I adore my husband and my kids—no complaints there. But I really think God owes me an explanation. Some of my friends say that the accident happened so I could have the three children that Rick and I are raising now. I don't see the logic in that. I refuse to believe I had to lose two amazing kids to turn around and have three more amazing kids. Why couldn't I have raised all five of them together? I was certainly willing, but that wasn't how it turned out.

In the aftermath of our tragedy, some friends said they couldn't imagine what Rick and I went through, and I said, "Good. Don't even try. It was hell. Just go and hug your children and be grateful for every moment you have with them." To this day, when I'm in a grocery store or a restaurant and I see parents yelling at their kids, I want to rush over and remind them that their children are alive so they really have nothing to yell about.

When the catastrophe was still fresh, when I was out of my mind with pain, grief, and devastation and I felt like I couldn't live a day without my beautiful children, I wondered why God had allowed this to happen. I never believed that God created this accident to kill my children, but I believed in miracles, so I needed to know why He didn't *stop* it from happening. I believed I was a good person. Why wouldn't He give me a miracle? And if I couldn't blame God, whom could I blame? I knew that David Raemisch, the drunk driver who plowed into us, was to blame, but I wondered if I could have somehow avoided it.

I was still in the bargaining stages of my grief when I promised God that I would do whatever He wanted in the future if He would just let me redo that one day. I bargained with Him in every way I could imagine. I even begged Him to let me die too so I could be with my kids, but He refused my requests. I was pretty angry with Him for a long time, and I thought I was being punished. I even thought about having a conversation with the devil to see if *he* would give me what I wanted, but I had to finally acknowledge that the God I know doesn't punish.

When I think back to the worst day of my life, the day I lost my two beloved children in a split second, the fact that a minute or so earlier, I noticed a stain on the front of my shirt and didn't speak up about it seems incidental. *How petty can you get?* you might be thinking, when the big picture of that day was so overwhelming and life changing. But as the saying goes, the devil is in the details. I remember being in the car with my family that Sunday afternoon, on my way to the mall, staring down at a spot in the center of my white shirt, wondering if I should ask Rick to turn around so I could change. We hadn't driven very far, and going back home would only take a few minutes. It must have gotten stained during our move from West Bend to Waunakee about a month earlier.

Rick had been offered a job to run an insurance agency in Waunakee, about an hour and a half drive from West Bend. Although we liked living in West Bend, this was an opportunity we couldn't pass up. It involved a promotion for Rick with a six-figure salary, a lot more than he was earning at the time, which would enable us to make ends meet without so much stress. And the school system in Waunakee was preferable to that of West Bend, the place where we had raised our kids. Drugs were starting to show up in the high school there, and we wanted something better and safer for our children, Joshua and Jessica, who were seven and nine years old, respectively.

From the moment my children were born, being a mother felt like the most natural thing in the world to me. The baby-in-diapers stage wasn't my favorite. It was too much work. But once they got a little older, I happily dropped into full-on mothering mode, driving them to soccer games, making their food, leading the Girl Scouts, and showing up for anything else that had to do with the kids and school. In fact, I took to mothering so naturally, I couldn't—and I still can't—imagine anything that would suit me better. When I talk to a child, I lean down to get on his or her level, and I have to admit that sometimes I'm more interested in children than I am in adults. To this day, kids who have just met me jump into my arms for a hug. I'm drawn to them, and they're drawn to me right back. I like talking to children, listening to them, and playing with them. Being a mother is just a huge chunk of who I am. So when I lost my first two kids and my identity as a mother, I had to wonder who I was without my children. How could I possibly get through life without them? Was it even worth trying?

I sometimes get chills remembering a time when Joshua was about three. I turned to Rick and said, "Josh is an old soul, and he isn't going to be with us for long."

"How do you know that?" Rick asked me.

I really didn't know how I knew. I tried to explain by saying, "Look at how big his ears are. He isn't on this earth for long." I'd heard that people's ears continued to grow throughout their lives, and Josh already had really big ears.

Rick thought I was just being a nervous mom. I told a few of my friends that I thought Josh might be destined to leave here before we did, but none of them paid any attention. I tried to push it out of my own awareness—it made me really uncomfortable—but Josh's degree of maturity was unusual. As hard as I tried, I couldn't keep him occupied with the normal things that delighted other children. He once ran in from outside to ask me, "Can I tear the lawn mower apart? I want to make something." I just couldn't find enough ways to keep him busy. I would go into his bedroom at night to stroke his cheek when he was asleep, wondering why I felt like his time here on earth was limited.

I was sure that Jessica, on the other hand, would be sticking around for a long time, and I did everything I could to keep them both safe. We talked about gun safety, and I told them, "If you're at a friend's house and they have guns, leave immediately and come back home." We talked about fire safety too, and we bought a minivan that would protect the kids in the event of a head-on collision. But it seemed that despite our best efforts, destiny had something else in mind.

On that fated Sunday, July 18, 1999, I returned home at about one o'clock after being away for the weekend. Rick had stayed home to take care of the kids, which he was happy to do since he'd been gone all week, working in the main office of his insurance company in Iowa. While he stayed home that weekend, two of my girlfriends and I went to Madison, Wisconsin, to take advantage of a big sale on dolls and their accessories at the American Girl store. These American Girl dolls were very popular with young girls, and Jessica was turning ten on September 24. Christmas wasn't all that faraway either, and she loved the American Girl store more than just about anything. The items there were pricy, but they had this great sale every year, so my friends and I left on Friday for a girls' weekend.

The sale started early on Saturday, and after we shopped, we went out for a great dinner. We shopped the sale again on Sunday. Because of Rick's new job, I had more cash available; I must have spent $400 before we were through. When we got back shortly after noon, Jean, the mother of Jessica's best friend, Melissa, dropped me off at home. I stacked my purchases on the front porch so Jessica wouldn't see them.

When I walked in the front door, the first thing I heard was, "Mommy's home! Mommy's home!" My kids came running down the stairs and literally attacked me, hugging me as hard as they could. There was nothing better. We had missed one another, but I had to ask Jessie to go hide in her room so she wouldn't see what I had bought for her. Her face lit up. When she ran downstairs to her room, Rick followed her, while Josh carried in a large hope chest that I had bought for Jessica's favorite doll, Josefina from Mexico. The engraved wooden chest was a place to keep the doll's clothing and the rest of her things.

Josh carried it to our bedroom and laid it on the bed, and then he went back and got the rest of the stuff from the front porch. He stayed in the bedroom with me while I unpacked the gifts. He really loved his big sister, and he couldn't have been more excited if the presents were for him.

People used to tell me I was lucky that my kids got along so well, that they were best friends, that they didn't fight. People noticed how inseparable they were. But it had nothing to do with luck. Rick and I raised them that way, teaching them to appreciate each other and treat each other with respect. We let them horse around a little bit—kids like to do that—but we never let it escalate until they were fighting. I won't have that in my house. I made sure they understood that we were family and we all needed to support and care for one another.

I started emptying the bags from the sale, laying the gifts on my bed and checking my list of who was going to get what. I had bought things for my mother to give Jessie and her other granddaughters. I had also bought things for my nieces. I was busy sorting everything out and making piles when I picked up a little orange basket with a black-and-white chicken with a red crest and a white fluffy tail sitting on wood chips.

"Josh," I said, "I bought this for your cousin Amanda, but Jessica loves her doll Josefina, and this accessory goes with her. Do you think Jessica would like the chicken in the basket?"

"Yes," Josh agreed, "she *would* like the chicken in the basket."

It landed in Jessie's pile.

Rick

While Beth and Josh were organizing the gifts in our bedroom on the second floor, I was admiring Jessie's room. I'd asked the kids to sort out their rooms and finish unpacking while Beth was gone, and Jessica was kind of a pack rat. She really had a lot of stuff, and she had spent that morning setting up her room exactly the way she liked it, arranging her knickknacks on the shelves so she knew where everything was.

"This looks great," I told her, admiring what she had done. "Are you excited that Mom went to the sale?"

She nodded enthusiastically. I told her she could have a new hamster since hers had died before the move, and we talked about building a few more shelves and moving a few things around. Jessie's new room had big windows; it was larger than her room in our old house, and it was the only bedroom on the lower part of our split-level home. She liked having some privacy since she was the older sister, and she loved the fact that she could walk down the stairs, take a short leap, and catapult herself straight onto her bed, which she did every chance she got.

Beth was sorting the gifts into piles, making decisions about them, and Josh was still with her when I walked up the stairs and into our bedroom. "Hey, you two," I said, smiling at the stacks of presents. "I have to go to the mall. Jessie wants to come. I'm going to be busy all week, and I need to build a fence for the puppy. I'm going to Menard's and see what materials they have so I can figure out how to build it. Why don't we all go?"

Jess and Josh with Nicki, their new puppy

I found out later that Beth didn't want to go to the mall. She didn't want to go anywhere because she'd been gone for a few days, and staying home appealed to her. But she figured that maybe I needed to get out since I'd been home with the kids all weekend. I'd spent some time on my new computer from work, checking the programs, and I had played with the kids a lot. But now we needed a fence so Nicky, our new puppy, could play outside. Sadie, our yellow lab, was five years old and relatively calm, but Nicky had sharp little teeth, and she loved leaping up onto the couch. So Beth changed her clothes, and we all piled into the Dodge Caravan minivan for a family trip to the mall.

Before we pulled out of the garage, Beth and I both looked in the back to make sure that Jessie and Josh had their seat belts fastened. Both kids were sitting in the third-row seat. Josh was sitting behind me, Jessie was behind Beth, and the middle seat was still in the garage. I had taken it out for the move so we could pack the van with boxes. The kids were looking at an *American Girl* magazine, and Jessie showed Josh what she hoped her mother had bought her. He just smiled; he refused to spoil the surprise. I pulled up into the last intersection before the beltway, waiting for the light to change so I could drive straight ahead. We heard sirens in the distance, and we were trying to figure out where they were coming from. The light turned green, and the two cars ahead of us pulled out into the intersection. I was about to do the same thing, but I hesitated a moment and then pulled out. The next thing I heard was a thunderous bang. It felt like an earthquake, and in that split second, our lives as we knew them died forever, morphing into something so terrible we never could have predicted it in our worst nightmares.

2

Catastrophe

Beth

R ICK AND I met in 1983 in a smoky bar called Bagg End in West Bend, Wisconsin, where we both lived. Remember when they allowed smoking in bars? I was eighteen, and Rick was twenty. When I went up to the counter to order a beer, he was deep in conversation with a friend of mine named Jane, one of my coworkers at West Bend Mutual Insurance. Jane still wore seventies clothing. She was a little bit behind the times, kind of hippyish, and most of the other workers weren't very nice to her because she was different. But I've always believed in being nice to everyone, and when I greeted her at the bar that evening, I couldn't help but notice the cute guy beside her. It was Rick, my future husband. I found out later that her boyfriend at the time was Rick's martial arts instructor, and although Rick respected him as a teacher, it was obvious he wasn't treating Jane with respect. Rick was counseling Jane that she shouldn't ever let anyone treat her badly in a relationship.

I went back to my table and partied with my girlfriends, but I couldn't stop thinking about Rick. There was just something about him, but when I headed back to the bar to talk to him, he had left and so had Jane. I approached her at work the next day. "Who was that cute guy sitting next to you last night?" I asked her. "Does he have a girlfriend?"

"Oh, my God," she said. "Why didn't I think of that last night? Rick thought you were really attractive. You two would be perfect for each other. He's just breaking up with his girlfriend; she turned out to be kind of a psycho. You should go out together."

"Oh no," I said. "There's no way I'm going out with someone in the middle of a breakup. No, no, no. Especially if the woman is crazy."

"You'd be perfect together," Jane insisted. "I mean it."

"I said no," I repeated emphatically.

Despite my resolve, you could say we had our first date on St. Patrick's Day when we met up at Bagg End a week or so later for green beer. It didn't start out like a date, but we ended up at the same table, we started talking, and we left together later to go to a different bar. I was getting pretty tipsy, and when Rick drove me home, I invited him in. I was living with my mom and dad back then, so Rick and I sat in their living room on a love seat and talked until three in the morning. By the time Rick left, I believed I'd met my soul mate. I had split up with someone prior because he didn't have a broad view of life the way Rick did. It was obvious right from the start that Rick felt the same way I did about a lot of things, and when he promised to call me the next day and he actually did it, I knew I could trust him.

We started dating, and we were basically inseparable for the next few years. I thought about getting married, and I knew that I wanted to have kids. I wondered if Rick would be a good dad, but when I went to watch him teach a tae kwon do class for kids, I knew he was father material. So why was he dragging his heels about getting married? I really wanted marriage and a family, so when I threatened to start dating another guy who lived in Florida, Rick proposed. We got married in 1987. We were just so good together, and when I got pregnant, first with Jessie and then with Joshua two years later, I found my calling as a mother.

Rick was working in construction when we met, installing carpeting and vinyl, and he was also a helicopter pilot in the National Guard. When he left the construction business, he went to work in energy conservation until he made another move to work in insurance and financial services. I stayed at home with the kids before they were old enough to go to school. Then I became a certified nurse's assistant when they went to school full time.

Everything I did back then was for my children. Mothering came naturally to me, and while I considered going to college and learning a vocation, I decided against it. You could say I was kind of a dinosaur, because I quit my job at a time when stay-at-home moms were practically extinct. But I really wanted to be there for my kids, and I loved every minute of it. I loved being a Brownie leader and steering my kids along the right path so they would get along with each other and treat their friends with kindness.

I'm telling you all this to describe the degree of immersion I had in my children's lives when the disaster happened. My children were my heart and soul when I heard the loud crash in the minivan on that Sunday afternoon.

Our car spun around in the intersection. We bumped into another car, and when we came to a halt, I called out, "What was that noise? What just happened? Is everyone OK?"

I had no idea we had been hit. When no one answered, I turned around to make sure the kids were all right. I saw Josh first. He was lying forward on the seat behind Rick. His seat belt was still fastened. His eyes were wide open, and his neck was visibly broken. The cheek that I loved to stroke at night was ripped all the way back to his ear. He was gone; I was sure of that.

Panicked, I looked behind me to see Jessica hanging out the window above the sliding door. Her head had slammed against the glass, breaking through it; the bottom half of her body was still in the seat while the top half was dangling out the window. I quickly glanced over at Rick. It looked like he had passed out, but he was coming back, leaning against the window and moaning softly. Thank God he was alive. When I looked down at my own body, half expecting to see blood, all I could see was a tiny scratch on my left leg. That was the extent of it, which was odd because traditionally, the passenger seat, better known as "riding shotgun," is usually the most dangerous place to be in the event of an accident. I suppose it depends on where you get hit, but I must have been surrounded by angels. I could feel them, and it was as if they had encased me. How else could I have survived the crash and gotten away with so little damage? But why hadn't they surrounded my children?

I opened my door and stepped out onto the pavement. I was confused when I saw two police cars speed off, traveling away from us to the left with their sirens still screaming. They were the ones we had heard before the crash, and they must have been heading somewhere else. "Oh my God!" I cried out. "Someone help me! I need a doctor! I need a doctor!" As if on cue, a strong hand touched my left shoulder. "I'm a doctor, and so is my wife," a man told me. They had been at the intersection in their car, waiting for the light to change. They had seen the speeding car, and they had watched it slam into us.

"You have to get my daughter out of the car. Please," I begged them. "Look at her. She needs help." I knew that Josh was gone, but I thought there was still hope for Jessica. I wanted to try to pull her out of the car myself, but I was afraid I'd hit her head. I left it to the doctors. My world spun as I began pacing around the intersection, muttering to myself, "This is a dream, a nightmare. I have to wake up. Somebody, please wake me up! Why can't I wake up? Why am I not waking up?"

A man was cradling Rick's head with his hands when I wandered over to his side of the car. I had no idea how this man had gotten there, but he seemed to know what he was doing, as he warned Rick not to move until they determined if he had a concussion or a spinal injury, or if he'd broken any bones in his neck. I heard him telling Rick, "You've been in an accident. You passed out. Please stay still until we figure out what happened to you. I'm an off-duty police officer. I was walking by and saw the accident."

"Where's my wife?" I heard Rick ask.

"She's right here. She's been walking around. She looks fine."

"Josh is gone," I told Rick.

He couldn't see much because he was lying down, but I saw my words register in his eyes as he lay there, not moving.

"She's right. My son is dead, isn't he?" Rick asked quietly.

"Yes, he is," the police officer said.

They had gotten Jessica out of the car by then. I don't know who did it or how. The sliding door, the only one that led into the backseat, was completely bent, and the entire back end of the minivan was gone. Someone must have pulled her out through the back and laid her down on a grassy area beside the curb where the husband-and-wife medical team were trying to revive her. I walked over and stared down at my daughter. She still had a pulse as I knelt down and whispered in her ear, "You have to make it, Jessie. I need you. I can't do this alone. You have to make it."

I got back up and continued pacing, moving from Jessica to Rick to the other side of the car where Josh was lying on the seat. "I'm so sorry," I kept saying to him. "I love you, and I don't know what to do." I wanted to reach out and touch him, but I couldn't. He looked so odd, so foreign. I didn't see any blood on him; he looked perfect except for his torn cheek, but there was no doubt that he was gone. His neck looked broken, and that little sparkle in his eye, that glint that seemed like the sunshine, was gone from Josh's eyes. His spirit was gone, and his face looked flat and empty.

That was when I noticed a man stumbling around the intersection. He had been driving the car that hit us, a Ford Crown Vic, the size and weight of a police car, and he appeared unstable and confused but unharmed physically. In fact, he was fine. His cushy airbag had saved him, but ours hadn't deployed because he hit our minivan from the side. The impact of his car slamming into ours had sent us flying, and we had plowed into a red sedan. The driver of that car, a middle-aged man, stood on the curb, holding his arm, which turned out to be broken.

I tried to make sense of it all as I kept begging and pleading to wake up out of the nightmare that wouldn't go away. I felt like screaming. I was in enough emotional pain to warrant it, but that isn't my way. It was never my way. I'm a fixer, not a complainer. Instead of freaking out, I was racking my brain for a way to take care of things—to change things—but there was nothing I could do with this level of destruction. Only God could handle this, and I wasn't so sure He could deal with it either. Where the hell was He, anyway? Why hadn't He saved Josh? If He hadn't saved Josh, did that mean He wouldn't save Jessie?

It seemed like everyone had something to do but me as I walked back toward the grass where they were working on Jessica. *She could still come back,* I kept reminding myself. But when I heard one of the doctors comment that some of her brain matter was outside of her head, I knew it was very bad. I had never felt so alone, and I felt stupid—that I was afraid to touch my son, that I couldn't help my daughter, and that I was completely unharmed in the midst of so much devastation. I walked from one family member to the other, letting Rick know that Jessie was still breathing and apologizing to Josh over and over.

A light flash went off in my face. Someone was taking pictures. I squinted. I had no idea who was photographing our tragedy, but I thought it was unbelievably rude and inappropriate. If hell existed, then I was in it. "We need a helicopter," I said out loud to no one in particular, and then I heard a whirring sound in the sky. A Flight for Life helicopter that originally had been called to a different scene had changed directions in the air and was hovering above our accident site. We never used it. It turned out that an ambulance was a more efficient way to get Jessie to the hospital quickly, but it was up there, and it landed nearby and waited in case we needed it.

When I saw them carrying Jessie into the ambulance that had just pulled up, I told Rick I was leaving with her. I got into the front seat as we were spirited away to the University of Wisconsin hospital. To this day, I can't recall how Jessica's head or face looked. They had to have been smashed and bloody, but thank goodness, I blocked it out. I guess the subconscious mind is good like that, and it did me a favor.

As we sped to the hospital, I reached for my cell phone. It was in my pocket. Against the backdrop of a screaming siren, I called my parents.

I got my dad; he and my mother were living in New Mexico at the time, and she was out shopping in El Paso, somewhere up in the mountains. It's funny the things that you think about when you're in crisis. A thousand unrelated thoughts were flashing through my mind as I remembered a time when I was six; I needed surgery for some reason, and my mother was out shopping in Milwaukee.

"We were on our way to the mall," I told my father, "and we had a horrible accident. Someone hit us." I told him what I could. It was hard to form my words, but I knew that the sound of my voice was probably telling him the story without my having to say very much. While he hung up to try to find my mother, I called Jean, one of my friends who had been with me during the weekend.

"Hi, Beth!" she answered cheerfully. "I just got home. Wasn't it a great weekend?"

I told her where I was and what that wailing sound was. She was stunned and could barely speak. Our trip to Madison for the American Girl sale felt like another world. I'd have returned there in a second, if only I could turn back time. But try as I might, despite the months of bargaining in which I would engage in the future to convince God to let me have a redo, it seemed that no matter what I did or said or how fiercely I threatened, I couldn't make Him budge an inch.

Rick

I knew I was all right. I had passed out, and my head hurt a little bit, but the training I'd done to earn a fourth-degree black belt in martial arts had given me a pretty good understanding of my body.

"I don't know what happened. Can you tell me?" I asked the man who was holding my head.

"You were hit by a speeding car," he said. "There were several cars involved, and we're trying to sort things out."

Jessie had been laid out on the grass behind me where they were working on her, but I couldn't see her. I was aware of Beth wandering over from time to time. Josh was still in the car, and I couldn't see him, either, but when Beth told me that he was gone, somehow I felt like I already knew it. I couldn't imagine how I knew, but I wasn't surprised. Beth told me she was getting into an ambulance with Jessie, that there was still hope for her, and she would see me at the hospital. I wanted to get up and go with Beth. I knew she needed me, but while she and Jessica were being sped away, I lay still as the paramedics removed me slowly and carefully from the car and put a brace on my neck to immobilize me. A second ambulance was leaving with the driver of the Crown Vic, and several people lifted me onto a gurney and carried me into a third ambulance. They weren't taking any chances with me; they needed to assess how severe my injuries were. I was disgusted when I saw flashes going off. People were taking pictures of me—of the accident. *Idiots*, was all I could say to myself as I was carried inside the ambulance and set in place for the drive.

"Where do you want to go?" one of the EMTs asked me.

"What? How the hell am I supposed to know?" I said.

"We have to take you to the hospital. Which one?"

I glanced at his face to see if he was kidding. "I want to go where my family just went," I said in disbelief. "Where else would I want to go?" The word *idiot* seemed apropos in this situation as well, but I kept it to myself.

Being with my family was everything to me. It always had been. After Beth and I got married and I found out I was about to be a father, I made a vow that I would never be like my own father. He was an alcoholic, as was his father, and the drinking killed him and tore our lives apart. It was unfortunate that alcohol was such a major influence in my life. It killed my father's sister, too, my aunt, and I vowed not to get personally caught in that trap. I didn't. But now, as much as I had kept away from it myself, the negative effects of alcohol were still wreaking havoc in my life.

As we headed for the hospital where Jessie and Beth were just arriving, a paramedic was continuously asking me questions like, "What day is it? What's your name? Who's the president of the United States? What do you for a living?"

They were trying to determine the extent of my injuries and if I had any brain damage. I answered their questions patiently, hoping they would let me get up. All I remember about that ride is that in between questions, they kept reminding me that there was hope for Jessie and not to give up.

"Miracles happen," someone said.

As I was trying to piece together in my mind exactly what had happened and the sequence of things, it struck me how odd it was that two doctors, an off-duty policeman, and a helicopter had all converged at the accident site, right when we needed them. And still, I knew that Jessie wasn't going to make it. I hadn't seen her after the crash. I hadn't seen Josh either, but I knew that he had died, that Jessie was about to die, and that somehow, they were OK. The truth that they were gone—and they weren't coming back—was as clear as the piercing shriek of the siren as they sped me toward the hospital where my family and friends were about to converge.

3

Saying Good-Bye

Beth

WHEN WE ARRIVED at the ambulance entrance of the University of Wisconsin hospital, they unloaded my daughter and carried her into a sterile trauma room with blue walls. I followed them, but they wouldn't let me into the room. I didn't know where to go or what to do. I paced the hallways, waiting for Rick to arrive, praying with every ounce of strength I could muster that the doctors would work their magic and save my little girl. Joshua was gone, but if I could just have Jessica, I could be strong for her. If she was still here, somehow I would get through it because I had to.

They had assigned us a private waiting room, and I looked in when I was pacing up and down the hallways. So far, the room was empty because most of our family and friends lived in West Bend, a good hour-and-a-half drive away. Laurie, my older sister, was the first to arrive since she lived nearby. I was confounded when she told me, "I just saw the man who ran into your car. He was in the public waiting room."

"What are you talking about?" I asked her wearily.

"He was throwing up. I just saw him. Then they told me to come here."

I stared at her blankly. She didn't have her story straight. There was no way David Raemisch, the driver of the Ford Crown Vic that had plowed into us, was sitting in the waiting room. He had been brought by ambulance to the hospital, and he was in the emergency room. I found out later that my sister had seen David Raemisch's brother, who was so upset about what had happened that he was vomiting. But I really didn't care about him or his brother. They were the last people on my mind. In fact, I hardly thought about David Raemisch at all back then or at any time in the future. I figured that what he had done was between him and God. They could work it out. I just wanted to see Rick, whose ambulance arrived a few minutes later. They wheeled him into a cubicle in the emergency room and pulled a curtain around him for privacy.

Rick

They still wouldn't let me move. It was frustrating to lie there still, but I did my best to stay immobile as they continued to ask me questions, trying to make sure my brain was intact. In the meantime, they cut my clothes off me and dressed me in hospital pants and a shirt. I was OK physically. I knew my body well enough to be sure of that, and I wished they would let me get up. I hadn't seen Jessie at the accident site. They had insisted I remain prone, but I felt in my heart that she wasn't going to make it. I knew Beth would need me at her side. That was when I heard someone in the next cubicle, yelling in a drunken slur, "Why are you doing this to me? I didn't do anything wrong! Why aren't you helping me?"

It was David Raemisch, the murderer of our children. Someone had been insensitive enough to place me beside the man who had just killed my son and probably my daughter too. I tried to forget he was there and focus on getting my neck brace removed. That was what I was thinking about when a doctor arrived and stood at my bedside.

"I'm so sorry for your loss," he said.

"Thank you," I said. "I know Josh didn't make it."

The doctor cast his eyes downward and muttered, "Son of a bitch." He walked away. Now I knew that there was no hope for Jessie. He hadn't had the heart to say it, but Beth walked in a moment later.

"The doctor just asked me if he could stop trying to revive Jessie and let her go," she told me with tears in her eyes. "I told him it was a decision I had to make with my husband."

That did it. I couldn't remain lying down a moment longer. I carefully removed my own neck brace, and when I was sure that my neck and head felt fine, I stood up and took Beth's hand. "Let's go say good-bye," I told her as we walked down the hall together.

We stepped into the trauma room and told the doctor he could let Jessie go. We also told him we wanted to donate her organs, thinking maybe something good could occur from all of this, but he said she had been dead too long. When he finally stopped trying to revive her and he and his aides had left the room, there was a terrible silence. There was no blood on Jessica; they had cleaned her up, and even with a tube in her mouth and a bandaged head, she looked beautiful. Her entire body was wrapped up in a sheet, almost like she was a swaddled baby, and bandages covered her head wounds. Her eyes were closed, and Beth and I talked to her for about ten minutes, letting her know how much we loved her. We asked our kids to take good care of each other. We told Jessica what a good girl she was, and we reminded her that she and Josh had each other; they would never be alone. When we closed the door behind us, we knew that our lives had been altered beyond recognition. I wasn't a father, and Beth wasn't a mother anymore. We walked slowly into the private waiting room where family and friends had begun to trickle in.

When my mother arrived, the first thing she saw was a bloodstain on my side. They had hooked me up to an IV when I was in the emergency room, and I must have held my arm too close to my side. Besides the blood, my mother was trying to process the fact that she had lost her two grandchildren, whom she adored, and she began to fall apart. Even though she had been a nurse for many years and had seen her share of blood and trauma, she began to sob and moan. I spent some time talking her down, convincing her that I was fine. When she stopped crying and became somewhat functional, Beth and I walked around the room, which was filling up quickly, hugging our friends.

At some point, I realized that that the American Girl dolls and gifts were still strewn all over our bed. Jessica hadn't lived long enough to see them, and it would destroy Beth and me to have to look at them when we got back home.

"Do you think somebody could go to our house," I asked Beth's close friend Pat, "and clear everything off our bed?"

She said she would find someone or she would do it herself.

Beth

Everyone was crying and asking us if we were OK. I wasn't OK. I was pretty sure I never would be OK again, but I didn't try to explain that to anyone. I wandered aimlessly from person to person. A cross-section of the people in our life had gathered. Along with family and friends, some of Rick's coworkers were gathering too, all talking quietly with looks of shock and horror on their faces.

I looked around and realized I had something very heavy weighing me down. My children had not been baptized. I'd been raised Catholic, and I found the rituals to be comforting when I was a child. But as an adult, while I still had my faith and I believed in God, Rick and I didn't have our children baptized because we didn't believe in the concept of original sin. I didn't agree with the Catholic credo that we were all born in sin and children who were not baptized would be sentenced to live in purgatory for eons. That just didn't make any sense to me, and it didn't make sense to Rick either. He had been born Lutheran, but he didn't have much interest in organized religion. We both wanted our children to make up their own minds about something as personal as religion, and we were willing to help them do the research as a family. When the time came, they could decide for themselves. Then, if they wanted to be baptized, we would arrange it.

The bottom line for me is that I believe in God. I believe that the Ten Commandments are His laws. But I don't agree with how the church tweaks them in an attempt to control the masses. That's what Rick and I both believed back then, and we still do. We didn't go to church regularly, and we were surprised to see a priest among the people in our waiting room. Someone must have called him in to help, or maybe he wandered in as part of the hospital team. I believed that my kids were innocent. They were not sinners, and while I hoped and prayed that they were in heaven, I wasn't sure, and that made me really angry at the Catholic Church. Just in case purgatory was a real thing, Rick and I thought it might not hurt to have the priest issue the kids their last rites, which would grant them mercy and forgiveness.

Rick walked over to him and said, "My daughter is in there." He pointed to the area beyond the double doors. "She just died," he continued, "and I don't know exactly what you do. But can you take care of her? Can you go do what you do?"

He nodded and headed for the emergency area to bless Jessica. Rick and I were just standing there, stock-still for a moment, with no direction or idea what we should do next, when my girlfriend Pat came up to hug me.

"Someone's on their way to clear the things off of your bed," she said. "Is there anything else I can do for you?"

I considered that for a moment. "Take me back to yesterday," I said.

She looked at me helplessly, and I thought back to the morning. Those few hours earlier felt like a century ago, when I had felt happy and carefree and thought my kids, Rick, and I had all the time in the world. I always hoped and prayed that we would watch them grow up and become adults. We would see them graduate, get married, and have our grandchildren. I remembered them rushing down the stairs to hug me after my weekend away, and I could still hear their sweet adolescent voices practically singing, "Mommy's home! Mommy's home!" I missed the hugs, their little voices, and seeing the world from their eyes.

My thoughts were interrupted when a policewoman approached us. "We just brought Joshua here," she said.

"Oh good," I told her. "I need to see him. I have to close his eyes. For some reason, I couldn't do it when we were still in the car. I have to hug him, too."

Rick and Pat wanted to come with me. The policewoman stopped us and said, "I'm so sorry. You can look at him, but you can't touch him. He's evidence."

"What?" I said in disbelief. "Josh is evidence?" *He's not evidence. He's my son,* I thought.

I think the policewoman repeated her admonishment—I'm not really sure—but I can hardly believe that I did as I was told. I just couldn't imagine walking in to see Josh and not being allowed to touch him or close his eyes. It would be better not to go in there at all, I decided, so I didn't. But when I thought about it later, I should have said, "I have to see my son, lady, so get out of my way," or I should have nodded and then did what I wanted to do.

Instead, I decided to be a good girl and do as I was told, a decision that I regretted for a long time. I understand now that I was in no mood to stand up for myself right then. I was in shock, and I wanted somebody, anybody, to point me in the direction of what I was supposed to do.

"Sorry to have to bother you," said the off-duty policeman, who had held my husband's head. He was now in full uniform,. He was standing beside us. "I need to get a statement from each of you if you think you can manage it," he said. He ushered us to a few chairs in the corner of the waiting room, and we all sat down.

We told him what we remembered, which wasn't much, and he offered to tell us what he knew so far.

"The man who crashed into you, David Raemisch, was fleeing the scene," he began. He went on to explain that he was speeding, probably going close to eighty miles an hour, when he ran over a bump in the road, which caused his car to go airborne. It crashed down onto the back of our car, broadsiding us and killing our two children. "We believe there was alcohol involved," he said. "You could smell it on him, and you could tell by the way he was acting. He couldn't even walk when he got out of the car. He actually fell over, but he wasn't hurt. We won't know for certain that he was intoxicated until the blood toxicology report comes back, but we're pretty sure." He added that a red car had been hit also, and the driver had sustained an arm injury. Nothing like this had ever happened before in this community, a small town called Middleton, a suburb of Madison.

We found out the rest of the story later. It seemed that David Raemisch's estranged wife had called him that morning and told him that she wasn't interested in getting back together with him. Distraught, he bought several bottles of alcohol, drove over to his parents' house, and after he had handed his parents his car keys for safekeeping, he had proceeded to drink himself into an alcoholic stupor. His plans went awry, however, when he got so drunk he started tearing up his parents' house and threatening suicide. Afraid for his son's life and for their home, his father called 911.

When a very drunk David Raemisch learned that the cops were on their way over, he'd asked for his car keys because he wanted to get out of there. When his father refused to hand them over, he grabbed his father's car keys without his permission, ran outside, got in his dad's Crown Vic, and took off. That was when he started speeding. The cops were en route to his father's house, responding to the 911 call. He had accelerated to eighty miles an hour in the middle of the city when he hit the bump in the intersection and broadsided our minivan. He still wanted to speed away, but when his airbag deployed, he couldn't drive anymore. He had stumbled into the intersection, tipsy, and he had been put into an ambulance. They had put him in a cubicle in the ER right beside Rick's. All the time he was denying that he had done anything wrong and asking everyone why they were treating him so badly.

When I think back, it seems like I should have been in a rage about him. But I wasn't. I was dumbfounded and in too much shock to have a normal reaction. My children were gone, and I had no strength to get angry or to strike out. That kind of behavior isn't in my nature anyway. I'm a private person, and I don't like to make a scene and attract attention to myself.

By the time we were through talking to the police officer, the waiting room was filled to capacity. People were milling around, trying to grasp the harsh reality of what had happened, and I remember someone asking me if I wished I had passed out like Rick did so I didn't have to see my children's bodies.

"No," I said, "I'm glad I was awake because I know for sure that neither of them suffered. They were hurt, but they didn't suffer."

A few hours had gone by when someone drove us home. When we walked in the front door, the house was full of people, and more were arriving. They had all come back to our house, and they were hugging us and trying to console us. The phone was ringing off the hook. Word was traveling fast, and I was grateful that someone had cleared off our bed. If the gifts had still been strewn there, I would have lost it completely. So even though it was strange and somewhat annoying to have a crowd at our home, if we had entered a quiet, empty house, it would have been more unbearable than it already was.

The rest of the evening is somewhat of a blur in my memory. I was aware that people were encouraging us to eat, but I couldn't. I knew food was important, that it had everything to do with our survival, but I wasn't sure I wanted to survive. I just held on to my husband for dear life and sat next to him when we all watched the ten o'clock news on TV. Thank God they didn't show any pictures of Josh and Jessica—I couldn't have taken that—but they showed the wreckage. Our relatives and friends who were watching with us were stunned when they saw the terrible damage that had been done to our minivan. They were surprised that we had survived. I was the only one who had seen it, since

Rick had been lying on his back with his head immobilized and hadn't seen anything when they put him in the ambulance.

When the news was over, we went to bed. What else was there to do? My kids had been there that afternoon. I had touched them, hugged them, stroked their hair, and laughed with them, and now they were gone. Where did they go? I had always prided myself on being a happy person, grateful for my family and my wonderful life. Now, I was sure that I would never be happy again. My heart was gone. It felt like it had been ripped out of my chest, and I began to replay the incident in my mind. A doctor had given Rick and me a prescription for sleeping pills and advised us to take them that night, but we didn't get it filled. We just hung on to each other and lay in bed, stunned and confused.

I started to bargain with God. If I'd had an opportunity to make different choices, it would have turned out differently, I assured Him. Most likely, my kids would still be here, so could He just give me one do-over? He could work miracles, so why couldn't He give us one? I don't know how long I lay there, holding on to Rick as tightly as I could, replaying the worst moment over and over. I was still bargaining for the restored lives of my two children when I finally fell asleep and had a powerful dream.

4

Baby Steps

The kids and I are together in Jessie's bedroom. Josh is sitting beside me on the bed. He looks sad. I can tell he misses Rick and me, and he rests his head on my shoulder. I place my arm around him to comfort him, and Jessica's eyes get huge. She's concerned; she doesn't want me to be sad, and she's worried that Josh's sadness is bringing me down. So she starts to dance around and do goofy things to make me laugh.

Beth

THIS WAS THE first of many dreams I had after my children went to the other side. In these dreams, it was as if I had entered a different realm, a peaceful realm in which I could communicate with spirits. In fact, I could touch and hear them and carry on conversations. It was uncanny how the differences in their personalities were so clearly defined in each dream.

Jessica was our sweetheart. She made friends with everybody; she didn't ignore anyone, and she wanted everybody to be happy. When she was in the first grade, Rick and I attended a parent-teacher conference and her teacher told us, "Jessie is like a shining star. She's one of the best kids in the classroom." I couldn't have been prouder. The typical all-American girl, she loved Winnie the Pooh and her American Girl dolls, and although she was more cautious than Josh, she learned to ride a two-wheel bicycle when she was just four. It seemed that Tommy, a cute little boy who lived down the street and was two years older than Jessie, could ride a two-wheeler. She wanted to do that too.

Jessica had a lot of friends, and she loved being with them. At the end of a sleepover party for her ninth birthday, I could tell something was bothering her. After we dropped the other kids at their houses the next morning, we were on our way back home when I asked Jessica what was wrong.

"It was hard," she said, "because I wanted all the girls to be happy, but they all wanted to do different things. I couldn't get them to play together, and it made me feel upset."

That was who she was. *Note to self,* I thought, *never throw a big birthday party like this for Jessica again.* She was so anxious to please everyone, she reminded me of myself, and I kidded with her. "I'm going to make T-shirts that say, 'I survived Jessica's ninth birthday party.'" She laughed, and so did I. Unfortunately, it would be her last birthday and her last party.

Jessie loved being active. She was always outside playing, running with the dogs, swimming in our pool, and jumping on the trampoline. She had no problem hanging out with Josh and the other neighborhood boys, and at the same time, she was a real girl. She liked cuddling with her stuffed animals, and she loved to play with her dolls. And like a good older sister, she always looked out for Josh, making sure he was OK and helping him whenever he needed it.

Joshua could become frustrated at times because his mind was advanced well beyond his years. He seemed to think he was capable of doing things that were impossible for his body. It was partly because he was a big kid for his age. As I said earlier, I always knew he was an old soul. He was very energetic. He loved playing sports, and at the same time, he was perfectly happy being alone. In fact, he could entertain himself for hours in the backyard, kicking around a football or playing with a baseball. Jessica had been my first child, and I'd spent a lot of time trying to keep her entertained, playing with her and making sure she had plenty of friends around. Joshua, however, was content to play by himself. He loved tinkering with things, and when he wanted something, he was like a bulldog that wouldn't let go.

I sometimes wondered if I'd made a mistake by entertaining Jessie so much. Maybe if I'd encouraged her to spend more time alone, she might have been more comfortable with it, like her brother was. However, I think they simply had different personalities.

Rick and I taught our kids to show their love by playing nicely with each other and with Sadie, our yellow lab, and Nicky, the puppy. The kids didn't fight or bicker, and they treated each other with loving-kindness because we showed them how. So the dream I had the first night they were gone reflected a great deal of who they were and how they looked at life. They were almost always together. Joshua was serious and thoughtful, and Jessie loved to make everyone smile—just like in the dream.

Joshua had an endearing habit of waking up in the morning, getting out of bed with his eyes barely open, and crashing into everything. We used to hear him banging into things and say to each other with a smile, "Josh is up." I wished he wouldn't crash into things, but on that first morning, when we woke up to a silence as deep as the ocean, I'd have given anything to hear him crashing around. My mornings in general were tricky once the kids were gone. I would wake up and have about ten seconds of ease, blissfully unaware of the tragedy that had devastated my life—until the accident came roaring back into my consciousness and the sadness took over. Reality hit me like a sledgehammer that first morning as Rick and I stared at each other, stunned by the silence. Josh wasn't crashing around. Jessica wasn't playing with Sadie.

The tears began running down my cheeks as I told Rick about my dream.

It was so typical of Jessie to worry that Josh was sad and want to save me from worrying about him. "Why didn't we die instead of them?" I asked Rick. "Life is so cruel. Nobody should watch their kids die. I don't think I can go on. I just can't do this for the rest of my life. I can't live without them. I can't get out of bed. I don't want to live without them."

"Can you just make it through today?" Rick asked me.

"No."

"Can you make it through the next hour?"

"No."

"What about the next five minutes?"

"No."

"Well," Rick said, "let's just try for a minute. Sit here and breathe with me, and let's get through a minute together."

Rick held me close, and we lay in bed just breathing together. I vowed never to get up again—until I suddenly had to go to the bathroom. Life came and got me, no matter how much I wanted to avoid it. I really wanted to avoid just about everything right then. But I got up and started going through the motions of life.

Rick

We had to focus on the very short term at first, taking baby steps, dealing with one minute at a time. Beth didn't want to get out of bed, and she'd say, "I don't want to get up, but I have to go to the bathroom."

I'd say, "Then go ahead."

"But I don't want to get up," she repeated.

"Well, you have to get up, or you'll pee in the bed."

Or Beth would say, "I'm not hungry, but we have to eat."

"I guess we do," I'd agree.

"But I don't want to eat," she'd say. "I have no appetite, and I really don't want to go grocery shopping."

"How about eating something really light, like a piece of cheese?" I'd suggest.

Or she'd say, "I'm exhausted, but I don't want to go to sleep."

"I don't either," I'd agree. But our bodies were tired, and the next thing we knew, we had dropped off to sleep. Life just had a way of interrupting us, especially when we wanted the world to stop. I remember saying to Beth, "The car is totaled. We need to buy a new one."

"I don't want to buy a new car," Beth said.

"I don't either, but we have to," I reminded her. "How will we get around?"

"I don't want to get around. I can't bear dealing with people."

On the second day after the accident, we stood out on our patio off the kitchen and watched the cars whizzing by. People were on their way to work or to drop off their kids, like we used to do.

Beth exhaled hard and said, "My life stopped, but people are driving around out there, going to work, doing their lives as if nothing happened. How can they do that?"

You can see that when I say we were taking baby steps, I mean *baby* steps. It was all about rebuilding our lives when we didn't want to, because we were having terrible moments that felt unbearably cruel. Although Beth and I never left each other's side for very long during those initial days, we felt excruciatingly alone as we recollected short tidbits of memories about things we did with the kids, places we went, and things they said. It hit me hard that there would be no more new memories, no more playing with them, hearing them laugh, smelling their hair, and putting them to bed. I missed all of those moments, and I also missed imagining what and who they would become. We flip-flopped a lot during that time, trying to be there for each other, taking turns at being strong and then being vulnerable.

When I look back now, fifteen years later, I realize that although we both were in terrible pain because of the tragedy, Beth had a harder time of it than I did because of our childhoods. Mine had taught me not to expect much and to move on when things were unmanageable, which was most of the time. I grew up with an alcoholic father who was unpredictable, so I learned not to expect good times.

My father was a self-employed electrician, and so was his father. While my grandfather was still alive, he and my father had the largest, most successful electrical contracting business in Port Washington. They were smart and well off until alcohol tore the whole thing apart. That was when expecting and accepting hardships became normal to me. I had three siblings, and we were never sure if we were getting presents on Christmas or on our birthdays. We all learned the hard way that we couldn't change what was going on, so we needed to accept it and deal with it, whatever it was. In other words, if you have no expectations, you have no disappointments. I was living in an environment that was completely out of my control, especially when it came to my father's moods.

I have to say here that there were a few things my father did that made a good impression on me. He taught me to do electrical work, which I teach my kids to do. But my father yelled a lot, and most of the time, he wasn't present, because he was always trying to figure out where his next drink was coming from.

For example, we would plan a family vacation and all of us kids would get excited. We'd pack our bags and pile into the car, and my father would start driving. But we didn't get very far, because he stopped at various bars along the way. We waited in the car while he drank, and when he got sufficiently drunk, everything would begin to spiral downward. He would stagger back to the car, useless, and my mother would take over, trying to keep the family together. She usually had to drive us back home while my father was yelling at everyone or just passed out.

We moved a lot when I was young, as many as twenty times, because my parents kept separating, trying to reconcile, and then separating again. I became so used to having my world upset that I didn't expect stability. I guess I learned to take the turmoil in my stride, which was the gift of having a childhood like that. So while losing the kids was agony for both of us, I was better at rallying and accepting life on its own terms than Beth was. She'd had a loving childhood, and she didn't expect bad things to happen. Her family all went to church together, and she had been a happy-go-lucky kind of girl who always looked on the bright side. With the exception of the "teasing and occasional harrasment she got from her brother, she expected wonderful things and lots of love, and that was what she got.

Beth

One of my biggest obstacles in life is paying attention to my inner voice or my intuition, speaking up, and getting other people to listen. For as long as I can remember, I've had very strong feelings about many things in my life that I attribute to an inner knowing. It's a voice I can hear that is strong and clear when it comes. But convincing other people that my intuition is right is another story.

A really good example is what happened two days after the accident. Rick was involved in martial arts, and one of his instructors, Fred, who was basically in charge of his training, was also a lawyer. After the accident, the people around us encouraged us to call a lawyer to see what our options were. We didn't want to go that route, but we figured it couldn't hurt to ask, so Rick called Fred.

Fred agreed that it was important to get things in place and make sure all the evidence was available in case we went to trial. I kept telling them that we didn't need a lawyer because we weren't going to trial. "Our case is going to settle," I said, based on the fact that there were so many witnesses and the tragedy of the outcome.

"There's no way we're going to court," I told Rick.

But Rick didn't listen to me, and neither did anyone else. Fred kept telling us that we needed to be protected legally. He said that because he was so close to us, he couldn't really handle our case himself, but he would put his partner, Rob, in charge. "Rob is much better at this kind of thing than I am anyway," he added. He told us that Rob was willing to take a third of our payout, which meant we didn't have to give him any up-front money.

"What if we don't go to trial?" I said.

We had no idea what kind of money we were talking about, but Fred kept reminding us that if we just signed the contract to give a third to the lawyers, we wouldn't have to pay a penny out of our pockets. Rick was willing to go along with it, but I said no. I told him he needed to hear me out and pay attention to what I was saying. I suggested that if anything came up, we could pay the law firm hourly. If there was a payout at the end, I just didn't see why anyone else should profit from our terrible loss.

But no matter what I said, Rob wouldn't back off. He kept trying to get us to sign his contract, and it turned my stomach. I got really pissed off that he was pushing us. It was rude, and I kept telling Rick, "These guys are ambulance chasers. We don't need to sign a contract giving them a third."

Fred repeated, "You need representation. You need to sign this. You don't want to get caught without a plan."

I kept saying, "No, we don't need to sign anything. There are two dead kids with their seat belts fastened and one drunk. I wonder who's guilty. It isn't going to trial." I kept telling them we just needed to pay an hourly rate. Even the victim assistance coordinator from the DA's office told us this would most likely be settled out of court, but in order to stop the pressure, we signed the lawyer's contract against my better judgment. I had no strength left in my body and no will to keep arguing. I just couldn't fight anymore, especially with Rick going along with them. He couldn't imagine that Fred or Rob would take advantage of us.

Once we had signed the contract and the lawyers went away to start placing all of our ducks in a row, I put the whole thing out of my mind. I had a lot to do to prepare for the funeral, and I decided to call Kathy, our psychic friend, whom we had consulted before our move. I had decided to get validation from Kathy that our move was a good idea, and when she agreed that it was, I felt like I was making the right choice.

If you're thinking that seeing a psychic is not normal for someone like me, a woman who considers herself a Christian, you're right. But the longer I live, the more I have come to understand that Rick and I are not what you would call a "normal" couple in any way. We look normal, and we want the same things that anyone else wants: peace, happiness, and a healthy family. But as a friend of ours once said, as far as being normal Midwesterners is concerned, we're kind of in disguise. I believe in God, but I also believe that He gives everyone his or her own special gifts. And He doesn't make mistakes. That's why I had faith in Kathy as a psychic. I felt it was a God-given talent, I still do, and I believe wholeheartedly in the spirit world. So when Kathy condoned our move, even though I still felt apprehensive about it, I believed that as long we were all together, everything would be OK.

Now I needed to quiet my mind, and I was hoping Kathy could help me with that. I couldn't have been more on point when I dialed her number, since unbeknown to us or to her, she was about to give us the biggest gift we could ever hope to receive.

5

Minute by Minute

Rick

ETH LEFT KATHY a message that we wanted to see her. She lived in West Bend, where we would be holding the visitation for our children on Thursday and then the funeral and burial on Friday. We hoped she could fit us in for a reading Thursday morning before it all started. For now, we had to meet with the insurance adjustor at the police compound where we would be getting our things out of the minivan.

I can't recall who drove us because so much of that time is fuzzy. I do remember that Beth and I were both filled with dread on the way over there. I had seen the damage to our car on TV after the accident, but since I had been lying on my back until I went to the hospital, the real impact didn't hit me until I was standing beside it. It was a terrible sight to behold. You could see where the windows had been broken, and one was partially gone from when Jessica was thrown against the side of the car. Her head had broken the window. It looked like somebody had taken a sledgehammer and hit the side of the van, ripping off the back end, which had completely caved in. There was the *American Girl* magazine, just lying there, the one that the kids had been looking at only one day earlier. *They were sitting right there,* I thought. *They were alive and laughing and looking at the magazine together.*

They hadn't been gone for twenty-four hours when I got my wallet and the DMV registration out of the glove compartment. It was agonizing to see evidence of the damage that had stolen our children from us. The back of the van was missing, and there was no question that the car was totaled when the insurance adjuster showed up. She couldn't believe that Beth and I were OK, and she was stunned to see that the passenger seat was intact. I have to say that she was very respectful to us, and so were the police. They both were amazed that we had survived the crash and even more amazed that neither of us had sustained any serious injuries.

"Comparing this car to others I've seen in the past," said the insurance adjuster, "you're both lucky to be alive."

But you could see by looking in their eyes that they were thinking, *These people have no kids. They're gone. They were taken away yesterday.*

Beth

We were all crying, and I couldn't get out of the police compound fast enough. The rest of the day crawled by. Time moved painfully slowly, and every hour was a trial to endure. I was living minute by minute, but Rick and I quickly found out we had made a great impact on the Waunakee community, even though we'd lived there for less than a month. We had been on TV on the day of the accident. During the following days, reporters covered the aftermath and the arrest of David Raemisch, who lived locally and was already out on bail. Everyone knew what had happened to us; the Waunakee community had started a memorial fund for us, and donations were pouring in.

We were moved by everyone reaching out to us, but we had to stop answering the phone. Each time someone asked us, "How did it happen?" or "How are you?" it reopened the wound, which was a long way from being healed. We just couldn't talk about it without falling apart. When I think back, I guess it was kind of insensitive of people to keep asking us those questions, but they were curious, and they were also at a loss. They really didn't know what else to say. Several of our friends told us later, "It was just too hard to call you. It was too hard to talk about it or think about it."

We just couldn't keep describing the accident, giving out the details or telling anyone how we felt. It was too painful to talk about it, and it was impossible to describe how we felt, so we let other people in the house answer our phone. They'd put their hand over the receiver and say, "Do you want to talk to so-and-so?" Sometimes we did, but most of the time, we didn't. If we were alone in the house, we let the calls go to voice mail. There were just so many, partly because the following e-mail was circulated by Rick's insurance company's home office to all of the agents the day after the accident.

> Tragic news. We received word late last night that Rick Olsen and his family were involved in a car accident Sunday afternoon. Rick and Beth are at home recovering from their injuries; however, their nine-year-old daughter, Jessica, and seven-year-old son, Joshua, did not survive the crash. No further information is available at this time. We'll let you know when we hear anything.

Rick

Beth and I didn't leave each other's sides. Sometimes we sat together out on our back porch off the kitchen, which had a sliding glass door. The house was split level, so we were raised about eight or ten feet off the ground. The day after the accident, I noticed a cardinal with bright-red feathers that kept landing on the railing. That was unusual for two reasons. First, the railing was so close to the porch where we sat—it spooked most birds to land that close to us—and second, although numerous creatures visited our yard all the time, we had never seen a cardinal there before.

I watched it whenever it landed. It usually stayed on the railing for ten or fifteen minutes, and then it took off. A while later, it would come back and land on exactly the same spot. Our friends noticed it and would say to me, "Hey, Rick, that cardinal is back." I'm not usually one to project meaning onto mundane things, but there was something about that bird that drew me to it. It was as if this beautiful bird was acting as a messenger, letting us know that someone was there in spirit, watching over us, telling us, "I'm here with you. I'm aware something huge is going on, and I'm supporting you." I started believing that the cardinal was there for a reason. Beth felt the same way, and when I asked around, someone told me that red was the color of love. We gave the kids a red tombstone for just that reason, and both Beth and I felt somewhat comforted when the cardinal was sitting on the railing beside us.

In those early days, while I tried to deal with what had happened, I realized that I had to change my frame of reference. Up to then, everything in our lives had revolved around the kids. Now that they were gone, I couldn't look a year down the road or even a month. I could hardly look at tomorrow, because imagining the future without Jessie and Josh was impossible. I had to deal with each minute as it arose. *Can I make it for five more minutes? Maybe. Can I build on that and make it for an hour? I can try.*

Beth

When we got back from the police compound, we found out that at some time during the day, Rick's mom had contacted a mortician. She had worked in the ER during her nursing career, and she'd gotten to know the ambulance drivers. Jim Phillip was one of them. He had stopped driving an ambulance and opened the Phillip Funeral Home in West Bend. He couldn't have been a more perfect choice. I had no idea that he would become such a pivotal influence in my emotional healing, but I liked the sound of his voice when we first spoke. I also liked the fact that he was willing to drive to Waunakee, pick up the children's bodies, and meet us at our house to make the funeral arrangements. I wasn't into going out. We were cocooning, shuffling around like zombies. Preparing to spend a few days in West Bend for the funeral proceedings, so I was relieved that Jim was willing to come to us.

Sometime in the afternoon on Tuesday, a station wagon pulled up and parked in front of our house. I didn't look outside; we'd been expecting a hearse, but when a man walked up to our front door and rang the bell, we figured it was Jim. We let him in, and the moment this tall, trim, handsome, brownish-haired man walked into our home, Rick and I felt a resonance with him, a sense that we could trust him. He was wearing cowboy boots; apparently, he and his wife liked horses. When Rick asked him where our children were, he said, "They're in the back of the station wagon. I don't like to drive a hearse around. It attracts too much attention."

He was my kind of guy. Rick and I led Jim downstairs to the basement where we had a rec room that we also used as an office. We sat, and he asked us to tell him a little bit about the kids. We told him some of our favorite stories. He had an easy laugh and a warm sense of humor that did not undermine the significance of what he was doing. He asked us about the funeral and what we wanted. He explained it was his policy to charge only his costs for children's funerals, so the expenses would be reasonable. We figured out that we would have the viewing of the bodies on Thursday at the funeral home and a shorter viewing before the funeral in Holy Angel's Church on Friday. And of course, the burial would be at the cemetery. We told him that we wanted to release doves at the grave site, and he liked that idea. When we asked for both kids to be placed in the same coffin, he said he had never done that before, but he would do everything he could to accommodate our wishes.

Jim told us he had the information for the death certificates and that he would need us to check them for accuracy. He handed Jessica's to Rick.

"It says the cause of death was decapitation," Rick said. "I didn't think their heads were cut off."

"No, they weren't," Jim said. "That's the medical term for a broken neck."

"Is that what they died from?" Rick asked.

"That and other things," Jim said.

Rick handed Jessica's certificate to me as he looked at Josh's. Jessica was born in 1989 on September 24, and her age at her death was nine years, nine months, and twenty-four days. The dates looked so similar that I questioned Jim about it. The more we talked about it, the more we realized that there was only one day in her life when those dates would match. She'd been born in 1989 in the ninth month on the twenty-fourth day. When she died, she was nine years, nine months, and twenty-four days old.

Before he left, Jim asked us what we wanted in the casket with the kids and what we wanted them to wear. We gave him some clothing and a few things that the children had loved. When he was about to leave, I said, "Can you please make sure Josh's eyes are closed?" I was haunted by the fact that I hadn't closed my son's eyes, but Jim reassured me that he would take care of it. I believed him.

When he headed back to the station wagon and drove away with our children's bodies, we knew we had chosen the right person for the difficult days that lay ahead of us.

The next days are a blur in my memory. One minute felt like an hour. I was in a constant state of bargaining with God. I just couldn't stop replaying the accident in my mind. Each night when I tried to sleep, I came up with a new proposition. If God would grant me one redo, I would tell Him, a redo of the day that my children were taken from me, I would do this or I would do that, whatever He wanted.

During those nights and for some time afterward, I would have dreams that Rick was dead. Sometimes he looked like a skeleton lying next to me, and I'd wake him up out of a sound sleep and say, "Are you OK? Are you breathing? Are you still alive?" But as hard as those nights were, mornings were worse. I would wake up to a deep silence in the house. I felt like I couldn't get through one more day, and I decided I needed some assurance that I would make it, that I could survive. I told my friends I wanted to talk to someone who'd had a worse experience than I did and had lived through it. Someone did some research and gave me a phone number for her aunt, who had lost her son and her husband in a car accident on the way back from a ball game. Four years later, she had lost another son in an accident.

I called her to talk about what she had gone through and how she had survived. I told her I had lost my two children in an accident, and I needed to know how to keep breathing and make it to the next day. She said a few comforting things, and when she began quoting Scripture to me, I didn't stop her. I listened, but I really wasn't talking to God right then. When I thanked her and hung up the phone, I felt slightly comforted. She had gone through a nightmare like mine, and she had survived. At least I got that much from her. But her way wasn't my way. I would have to figure it out for myself.

We made it through to Wednesday, five minutes at a time, hardly leaving each other's side as we prepared to head to West Bend in the late afternoon to put the children to rest. Kathy had returned my call, and when I asked her if she could squeeze us in on short notice, she said, "Of course I'll see you on Thursday morning. But I have to tell you that I feel badly about your last visit. I condoned your move. I encouraged you, and look what happened. I'm just so sorry."

I assured her we didn't blame her a bit. I believed there was no way she could have predicted what was going to happen. Kathy sounded relieved when we made arrangements to come and see her. When I think about what would have happened—or should I say, what would *not* have happened—if we hadn't made that appointment, I feel fortunate that we made the right decision. But I'm getting ahead of myself.

We left Waunakee in the early afternoon on Wednesday, heading for Jim Phillip's funeral home. We decided to go there first, to make sure everything was in order for the viewing that was scheduled for Thursday, the next afternoon. We didn't stop for food along the way, because both of us had lost our appetites. Food tasted bland to me. I felt a sense of dread as we approached the funeral home. It wasn't so much about Jim. Even though we had met him only once, I had a good feeling about him.

But when we drove into the parking lot of the funeral home, it just felt too real. We were there to talk about burying our children, who had been alive and well just a few days earlier.

When Jim met us at the door, I felt deflated and discouraged. But something he said took me by surprise. "Your kids," he said with a big smile on his face. "I just don't know. That Josh is a real trickster." He shook his head. "He keeps turning the lights on and off, and he's messing with my music. He keeps changing the radio station, and he won't leave my stuff alone. C'mon in."

"What?" I said.

Josh had always loved to tinker with electronics and music when he was alive. But now that he was gone, I was not prepared for the things Jim was telling me as we walked inside and sat down to talk with him.

"Could you ask him to stop?" Jim continued with a laugh. "I'm trying to work on him, and he's playing games with my music."

That was the first spark that maybe, just maybe, there was a way to still be with the kids. Maybe they weren't so far away after all. Maybe I could communicate with them, as Jim was doing. What if they *were* actually around, tinkering, playing with the lights like he said, making their presence known? I glanced at Rick, who looked as stunned as I felt. I didn't realize how pivotal that moment was at the time, but now I see that Jim was introducing us to our kids as spirits; he was sure they were still around. He was so sure that he was asking me to talk to Josh and tell him to stop playing with the music. Something was stirring inside of me as we went over the arrangements. Jim told us he had found a casket large enough to accommodate both kids. We headed over to my mother's best friend's condo. She had been kind enough to offer us her basement room for the next two nights.

We ate very little, and even though we were exhausted, neither of us slept very well that night. We kept waking up all night long. Maybe we were disoriented from being away from home, or we were just too upset about the funeral to rest. For whatever reason, I woke up on Thursday morning after a bad night's sleep in a great deal of emotional pain.

Neither Rick nor I discussed food. We didn't eat breakfast before we left the condo and began heading toward Kathy's house. I didn't know exactly what I wanted from her, but I knew it was important to visit her before we began an ordeal that was too painful to even imagine.

6

Chicken in the Basket

Beth

ICK AND I pulled up to Kathy's two-story brick home in West Bend. It was located across from a cemetery. She met us at the door. We all hugged and cried, and she led us down to her basement, where she did her psychic readings. It was an older house. The basement was concrete that had been painted, and the room was clean but pretty Spartan. We sat down on a love seat in front of a table and chair, and Kathy sat across from us. There were fresh flowers in a glass vase on the table, and some beautiful quartz crystals rested on a wall shelf to our left.

I didn't know what to ask Kathy as she began giving us some general information. It was similar to seeing a therapist. We talked back and forth about how we felt and wondered what she could see about our accident and our loss. I told her that we hadn't baptized Jessica and Joshua before they died, and I was scared to death that they might be languishing in purgatory. I don't know how she knew, but she assured me that was not the case.

I can't recall much more of what Kathy told us. I guess we talked for about an hour, and I felt somewhat comforted by her. But all that really mattered was the last five minutes when we were about to leave. We stood up to say our good-byes. We were getting ready to go to the viewing at the funeral home. My stomach felt hollow, and I was wondering how I would get through it when Kathy said, "Wait a minute. The kids are here."

We sat back down. "No, Jessie is here. Josh is at Great America," she said with a smile. She was referring to Josh's favorite amusement park, which was always teeming with people; you had to wait in long lines to get on the rides. "There are no lines at Great America in the spirit world," Kathy said. She tilted her head to one side as if she were listening to something. After a few more minutes, she asked us with a questioning look on her face, "Does Jessica like fried chicken?"

I couldn't imagine why she was asking that. "Not really," I said. "I never make fried chicken for the kids because it isn't all that healthy."

"Well," Kathy went on, "she's telling me that she wants the *chicken in the basket*. That's what she's saying. 'I want the chicken in the basket.' Does that mean anything to you?"

I didn't make the connection at first. I wondered what on earth Kathy was talking about. There was a product in the grocery store called Chicken in the Biscuit, crackers that tasted like chicken spread on a dry cracker, and it was terrible. Jessica couldn't have been referring to that. Then I got it. She was talking about the chicken in the basket from the American Girl store—the accessory that went with Josefina, Jessie's Mexican doll with the long dark hair.

I stared at Kathy and then at Rick. Neither of them knew a thing about the chicken in the basket that I had bought over the weekend. Rick had never heard of it, and besides the two girlfriends who were with me, only Josh knew about it. "Well," Kathy continued, "it's very clear. Jessie wants the chicken in the basket."

"It's for her favorite doll, Josefina," I said to Kathy and Rick with tears welling up in my eyes. "I bought it for her cousin, and I asked Josh if he thought Jessie would want it instead. He said yes, and now she just agreed. She wants the chicken in the basket! Oh my God. Josh and I were the only ones that knew about that conversation. They must have discussed it after they passed, and now Jessie is giving us the answer!"

I had given Jim the Josefina doll to put in the coffin with Jessie. Now, I called my friend Jean and asked her if we could have the chicken in the basket she bought for her daughter so we could put it in the coffin. When I hung up the phone, I realized that I had just received a communication from my daughter. My kids were alive! They may have left their bodies, but their spirits were alive and well. I knew for sure now that they weren't dead. And they definitely weren't in purgatory. For all the Catholic dogma that I had been taught, they also believed in eternal life, and that made sense to me right then. My kids were not only alive, they were OK, and they were with God. I glanced at Rick and saw that he was crying too. So was Kathy. There was no way she could have known anything about the chicken in the basket. Her own kids were grown, so there was no reason she would have been paging through an *American Girl* magazine. The communication had come directly from Jessica. There was no other explanation.

This moment was more pivotal than I can possibly express. It was the beginning of my ability to accept the reality that although my kids had been killed, they were still here. A euphoria came over me. I was grateful for the way Jim had described Josh. He had provided my entry into the spirit world with his descriptions of Josh playing with the music and the lights. I recalled him showing us around and pointing to a cross on the wall. "Look at that cross," he'd said. "It looks like normal wood, but when you stand over here, it shines. Do you see what I mean?" He was giving us tidbits about the magical quality of the spirit world. Jim was trying to explain that God had a design for everything, and He had been there at the accident and at the funeral home. I hadn't fully understood when it happened, but that had changed when I received a specific message from Jessie—a message about something that no one but Jessie, Josh, and I could have known.

I felt redeemed. I had proof—tangible proof. My kids were not gone. Although I could never touch them again or smell their hair, they were still around. I could talk to them, and they could talk to me. I knew for sure that my children were living in the spirit world, and in that moment, it felt like I had been saved.

"Jim Phillip, our funeral director, invited us to come stay at his small cabin in Colorado for as long as we want after all of this is over," Rick told Kathy. "He said it isn't much, but it's in the mountains, and it's very peaceful."

"We keep thinking about stopping the world for a while," I added. "We could go to Colorado, but maybe we should go to Hawaii. What do you think about that?"

"Hawaii feels wrong to me, but Colorado feels right," Kathy said.

I filed that for the future. Now, it was time for us to go, so we all hugged. When Kathy saw us to the front door, she told us, "The kids are arranging something special for you when you get in the car. Some sort of message. Watch out for it."

Rick

When Beth and I got into the car, it felt like we could see a lot more light. It was as if someone had thrown a switch and we had been renewed. I missed Jessie and Josh just as much as I had before, but now I believed that they were here and that they wanted to communicate with us. I had been preoccupied by the fact that everything Beth had asked for at the accident had showed up, including two doctors, a helicopter, and an off-duty police officer. She and I were both alive and unhurt when so many people thought we should have died. Jessica died on the only day that the numbers on her death certificate and her age could have matched up. And then I had paused several seconds before I entered the intersection after the light changed.

There had been divine intervention. I was sure of that. But could I dare to believe that the accident was meant to be? I wasn't about to say anything to Beth yet. She was having a hard time making it from moment to moment, from place to place. I didn't want to push her too hard too fast. But Jessie had communicated with us, and that made all the difference.

I started up the car. When I turned on the radio, a familiar song began to play. A couple of weeks before the accident, the four of us had gone to see the animated movie *Tarzan*, which we all loved. It was right up there as one of the kids' favorite movies. They especially loved the song we were hearing right then, "Two Worlds, One Family."

> No words describe a mother's tears,
> No words can heal a broken heart.
> A dream is gone, but where there's hope,
> Somewhere, something is calling for you.
> Two worlds, one family.

As we listened to the familiar lyrics, Beth and I cried with joy and heartbreak at the same time. Our kids were with us, and they had arranged for their favorite song to play on the radio. What a gift! Even though we were living in different worlds right now, we were still a family, just as the song said. Our children were communicating with us. I could feel their presence, and I was determined to find a way to send messages back to them.

I had driven a mile or so when I turned to Beth and said, "Are you hungry?"

"I am," she said. "Actually, I'm starving."

"Me, too," I said and smiled. "Let's grab a bite before the viewing." It was as if our bodies were telling us, *This is not the end. You can eat and go on from here.*

I stopped the car at Hardee's, a drive-through fast-food restaurant. I ordered a burger, and Beth got a roast beef sandwich. We were actually hungry when our food arrived. It was the first time since Sunday that we could taste our food, and we were smiling. It felt like somebody had opened a door and we were walking out of the darkness into the light. Our kids were not gone; we had tangible proof because they had sent us a message. Well, Jessie did. Josh must have said, "Hey, Jess, you handle this. I'm going to Great America."

While we were eating, Beth and I talked about what had just happened and how grateful we were for the gift that the kids had given us. "Let's keep it a secret," Beth suggested. "We don't need doubters. We don't need any Judgy Judgertons telling us it isn't possible." She had picked up that expression from a girlfriend, and no one could have described it better.

The truth was that whether anyone thought it was possible or not, it had happened. We had both been there to hear it and feel our children around us. I agreed with Beth that we would keep the chicken in the basket story just for us.

Beth

We were the first people to arrive at the funeral home. Jim greeted us and ushered us into the viewing room. "I found an oversized man's coffin," he told us, "and I still wasn't sure if I could fit the kids in there side by side. The width was the challenge because I didn't want them to look cramped. But it turned out that they fit perfectly. They fell against each other, and it was as if they snuggled right in."

I wasn't surprised. They had always loved being together. And yet, even though we had just communicated with Jessie, it was heartbreaking and devastating to see our beautiful children in the coffin with some of their favorite toys strewn around. I looked at Josefina, Jessie's Mexican doll. Jessie had on a pair of American Girl pajamas that matched Josefina's white pajamas with long sleeves and a little red bow. They both had on white socks.

Josh was wearing his green-and-gold Packers shirt that had the number 4 on it, Quarterback Brett Favre's number. He had on his favorite baggy jeans and no shoes. I had kept their baby blankets for myself, but they were lying on a couple of blankets that Rick's mother had made. We wanted them to look cozy and comfortable.

As we stared into the coffin, Rick and I were amazed at the reconstruction job that Jim had done. He had fixed Josh's cheek, which had been torn in the accident. It looked almost normal. And he had cleaned up Jessie's head. They both looked pure and unharmed. And as he had promised, Jim had closed Josh's eyes. I felt a sense of relief about that. Flowers were everywhere, sent by friends, family, and coworkers, and although the kids looked beautiful and peaceful, it was also heart-wrenching and awful to see them there. I wondered how people were going to react.

Our families were the first to arrive, and judging from the looks on their faces, this was going to be very difficult for everyone. They fell apart when they looked at our two beautiful children in the coffin together. It was hell for everyone; they all seemed to be stunned, and they were really questioning where God was. After all, we were a good family with wonderful children. Our families were questioning their faith, wondering how God could have allowed this to happen.

It was so sad to see how much they were hurting. Before any other people began to arrive, we gathered our families together in a side room and told them the chicken in the basket story. We had vowed to keep it to ourselves—it had felt good to have such a powerful message from our children—but our loved ones were so distraught, we thought maybe it would help them as it had helped us. I was right about that. I saw a giggle, a smile, and a sense of relief among some of our family members as we all went back into the viewing room. Jean had arrived, and she gave us the chicken in the basket, which we placed in the coffin next to the Josefina doll. I would love that accessory for the rest of my life.

When the viewing started, Jim told us to pace ourselves, to take breaks and make sure we didn't burn out, but we didn't follow his suggestions. There were too many people, literally hundreds of them, who showed up to view the children. A group of executives from Rick's business had flown to West Bend in the company jet to pay their respects, and Jim Phillip said it was the largest viewing he'd ever had in his funeral home. But it seemed like everyone who walked in was wondering, *How the hell could something like this happen?*

We were standing in the receiving line when we noticed some of our family members telling the chicken in the basket story to different people. I turned to Rick and whispered, "They're telling our story." I was upset that our precious secret was being told again and again. But as we watched peace wash over people's faces, I realized something. I said to Rick, "The chicken in the basket story isn't just for us. It's for everyone."

Rick nodded. I felt a little sad at first that our story wasn't going to remain private, that it wasn't just ours anymore. It had felt like a precious gift that I didn't want to share. But now, Rick and I were both satisfied that if it could help people, then it was important to let our family members tell whomever they wanted to tell. My father, nicknamed "the Town Crier," was letting people know that even though our children's bodies were in a coffin, they were also alive. It was like offering a reprieve to our friends and families, a way to accept the unacceptable. It was something to hold on to when it seemed like God had abandoned us. From what we were seeing, our story was meant to be told, so we let go and allowed people to tell it. That was when I knew that someday we would be telling the story to the world.

The viewing lasted longer than the scheduled three and a half hours. There was a steady stream of people, and it went on for an extra forty-five minutes because they kept arriving. We had to endure a lot of pain, as people didn't seem to realize what they were saying when they told us that over 90 percent of couples ended up divorcing when this kind of tragedy occurred. A few people mentioned that we were lucky we were young enough to have more children. We imagined writing a book called *Funerals: What Not to Say*. At the same time, we knew that people were at a loss, so they blurted out some strange things.

Rick and I never sat down. We were talking to everyone and hugging them, until Jim walked up to us for the third time. "You two haven't sat down all afternoon," he scolded us. "I keep telling you that you need a break. If you don't take one, I'm going to drag you both out of here."

Jim was scheduled to say a few prayers at the end of the viewing, which we didn't want to miss, but Rick and I were relieved to take a short break and go to the restrooms. We got some water to drink and splashed some on our faces, and by the time we came back, Jim had already started the prayers. We stood at the back of the room, closed our eyes, and joined with our loved ones who had gathered to help us put our children to rest.

Rick and I were completely drained by the end of the day. We drove to the condo where we would be spending one more night, and all I could do was thank God that Kathy had been able to see us. How else would we have gotten the gift that would restore our faith and enhance us for the rest of our lives? I thought I could get through just about anything now that I had received Jessie's communication, but we had another long hard day ahead of us with an hour-and-a-half viewing, a funeral, and the burial where our children's bodies would be put to eternal rest in the earth. That would be excruciating, but at least I didn't feel like I had completely lost them. It was pretty clear that while Jessie's and Josh's bodies would be gone, their spirits weren't going anywhere. They were alive and well and ready for the next phase, whatever that would turn out to be.

7

Honoring Our Children

Beth

E STOOD AT the back of the Holy Angel's Church on the day of our children's funeral. Hundreds of people had shown up, and the service was scheduled to begin soon when I noticed a young man standing next to the coffin. I approached him and asked him who he was. He told me he had been Jessica's substitute teacher in the third grade in West Bend, right before we moved.

I recalled that when the school year had started, I didn't like Jessie's assigned teacher. I thought she wasn't as good as some of the other teachers. I could have requested a different one, but I decided to say nothing and trust that the right thing would happen. I became aware that some of Jessica's classmates were pretty hard to control when Jessie got home from school one day and told me, "Adam is so naughty. He throws things around in the classroom. The teacher said we were supposed to get underneath our desks so we don't get hit by anything." It was midterm when the teacher in question had what they called a nervous breakdown—she simply couldn't manage the kids.

When she went on sick leave, they tried out several substitutes. The man with whom I was talking had started in January and stayed until the end of the school year. He had stuck it out, but right then, he wasn't very happy. "I feel terrible," he said with tears in his eyes. "Jessica was such a good girl. I didn't pay much attention to her. I had to focus on all the naughty children in the class, and I ignored her. She was just so good; I didn't need to do anything extra for her."

I felt as badly as he did at that moment—maybe worse. *You didn't pay attention to my daughter?* I thought. I was distraught that during the last year of Jessica's life, her teacher had ignored her. I could have homeschooled her and had her with me instead of at school where the teacher wasn't giving her any attention. It broke my heart that he had overlooked my daughter because she had been a good student and had behaved well. But I also realized it was sweet that he cared and in the future, maybe he would pay attention to every child. For me, it was one more item on the growing list of things I wanted to change but couldn't.

When the funeral was about to start, one of our family members placed a camcorder at the back of the room to tape the service. The church was completely packed, overflowing with people. Rick had been in the National Guard, based in Madison, and a large group of people who had served with him were there. So were Rick's current coworkers in the insurance industry as well as Jessica's Brownie friends and Josh's buddies from school. A man we knew who had become a police chief was crying his eyes out, and there were a host of people we had never met. They had heard about us and seen us on the news, and now, they were here. Some of our guests were comforting us; we were comforting some of them. So many people were looking at the coffin and shaking their heads. "Where was God?" seemed to be the theme of the day.

The death of my children was everyone's worst nightmare come true, and we were grateful that we had the chicken in the basket story to keep us going. When Kathy, our psychic friend, arrived, I walked her over to the coffin to see the kids, whom she was just meeting for the first time. She had brought some hope into our lives at a time when it felt like we had lost everything, and we were both grateful.

There were not enough seats for everyone to sit. It was standing room only at the back of the room, and I remember looking down at my flowing pastel dress that had a drawing of Winnie the Pooh on it. I wore it because Jessie loved Winnie the Pooh, and it seemed a lot more appropriate than wearing black. I looked at the enormous number of floral arrangements all over the church. How ironic that this was the same church where my parents had gotten married, and now, my family was sitting all around once again, but this time, we were crying tears of grief, not joy.

When the funeral began, the priest led us in some prayers and spoke for a while, and then several people got up to talk. It was hard to endure. They were all in shock and hardly knew how to express their feelings. I sat there, clutching the children's baby blankets to my chest, wishing it were over and I could disappear. When we finally walked down the aisle behind the coffin at the end of the service, Rick overheard a huge man, a former linebacker in the NFL, telling his friend, "I've never seen anything sadder than this in my entire life. And I don't think I ever will."

Rick

When the prayers were over, we escorted the coffin down the center aisle of the church. We had arranged for "You'll Be in My Heart," a song from the movie *Tarzan*, to play in the background, and people gasped when they recognized it. There wasn't a dry eye in the house, and as my gaze swept the crowd, I saw looks of confusion, pain, and sorrow on their faces. Here or there, someone was staring at us, wondering how on earth we were getting through this. I had no idea. We were just doing what we had to do, and I drew strength from remembering we had made contact with Jessica the day before. After what seemed like an interminable amount of time, people were still filing out of the church when Beth and I got into the hearse and headed for the cemetery.

Jim drove, the priest was in the passenger seat, and Beth and I were in the back. There were easily a hundred cars behind us, and it felt surreal as we heard Jim and the priest bantering back and forth. They weren't being disrespectful. They were both highly spiritual people who loved our children, but they had a rapport, and it was obvious they had done this kind of thing before. When Jim came to an intersection, he held out his hand and said, "Just like the hand of God, everybody stops."

The priest smiled.

It just wasn't possible that our children were in the back of the hearse, about to be buried, and Jim and the priest were smiling. It was almost as if they were saying, "Life goes on, no matter what happens. And we have to go along with it."

We finally turned on to the road leading to the cemetery. When we got to the grave site, we got out of the car and stood there a while. There were just so many cars arriving, and they were still pulling in when the service started.

Beth

On the drive to the cemetery, we were the lead car in the procession. I saw other cars stopping for us that were not part of the funeral. People who didn't know us were getting out of their cars to pay their respects. A few men had taken off their hats and were holding them over their hearts. I thought back to a day or so earlier when I had been out on the porch with Rick, watching people driving along the streets in their cars. I had said, "My world just came crashing down, and they're all out there driving along as if nothing were any different. No one is stopping to honor our children. Why is the world not stopping?"

Today, West Bend was stopping to honor our children as they stood there quietly, waiting for the long funeral procession to go by on this brutally hot summer day. It meant a great deal to me. I told Rick, "Look, the world is stopping for Jess and Josh."

The priest led us in a short service at the grave site. When he was through, Jim stepped up and said, "Rick and Beth asked me to release doves here that signify peace and freedom. I told them I would work on it. So now I'm going to release these pigeons because I couldn't get any doves." He kind of stumbled on his words, and a few people smiled a little bit. After the birds took flight one by one, we watched the coffin descend into the earth where the kids would rest together for eternity. Once again, Jim had done us a big favor that we knew nothing about at the time. He had put the coffin in a cement vault, because if we wanted to move it later (which we did when we moved to a different city), it had to be in cement. We hadn't asked—we didn't know there were different ways to do it—but Jim had made sure we had what we needed. It was a welcome gesture during this difficult time.

When it was over, we all got into our cars to meet back at the funeral home where we had to figure out what to do with the hundreds of bouquets of flowers that people had sent or brought with them. I remember my mother telling people they should take the floral arrangements and deciding which ones we should keep. She kept asking me, "Do you want this one? Who do you want to give that one to?" It was really hard for me to concentrate. The father of one of Josh's friends had a truck, and in the end, we loaded up the back with flowers, and he delivered them to several local nursing homes.

When we had finished all of our business and could get out of there, someone from MADD (Mothers against Drunk Drivers) suddenly showed up, out of breath, with a box of banners from their organization. We had called them after the accident and told them about the funeral and what had happened to our children at the hands of a drunk driver. They said that someone would show up with banners that could go on our car antennae. But by the time they arrived, their boxes of banners in tow, it was all over.

I felt bad for a moment, but when I analyzed the situation later, I realized that we hadn't really missed an opportunity because we weren't mad. I couldn't imagine flying a banner on our antennae or asking anyone else to do it, as if we were advertising something. I believe that God intervened; the funeral was about our kids, not about making people aware of an organization, albeit a positive one.

I can't remember what we did when we got back to the condo where we were staying. But I remember quite clearly that my parents expected us to go out with them for dinner that night in West Bend. They felt that we *should* be with family, but we wanted to be with our friends, some of whom had flown in from all over the country. So that was what we did. While it upset my mother that we weren't doing what she considered the proper thing, we were relieved to be with our friends. We even managed to smile once or twice that evening, and we talked about the chicken in the basket and how impactful it had been for us.

The following night, Rick and I succumbed to the pressure and went out with my family. They had made a reservation at Walden's, a supper club.

"You have to eat," my mother told us.

I wasn't particularly hungry. I didn't want to get dressed up, put on makeup, make sure my hair was combed, or choose an appropriate outfit. But I did it anyway. Maybe I felt guilty that Rick and I had gone out with our friends the night before. All I remember is sitting across from my niece and nephew at the restaurant, thinking to myself, *Why do some children get to live, and my children had to die? I hope they do something awesome with their lives.* I was out of my mind with the unfairness of it all.

When we got back to the condo for the last night, I really wanted to be back home. I was tired of hardly sleeping, keeping up a front, having to be strong for everyone, and dealing with requests from our families that didn't seem important to me. I needed to stop the world for a while.

In the morning, we would drive back home and start a new life. It was one that I didn't want, but it looked like I had no choice. As I lay down beside Rick to try to sleep that night, I did something that, unbeknown to me at the time, would become a ritual, a private one. I didn't even tell Rick about it, but each night to this day, after I've tucked in my family and I'm ready to sleep, I whisper, "Kiss, kiss," to Jessie and Josh before I drop off to sleep, in the hopes that they might visit me in my dreams.

8

Stopping the World

Rick

*W*E CURVED UP, up, up the narrowing roads into the Colorado Spanish Peaks in our new Ford Expedition. Although it had been the last thing we wanted to do, we had to get a new car, and neither Beth nor I had been in the mood for wheeling and dealing. I remember looking at the salesman, who was trained in salesmanship, and I said, "Wait a minute here. This is what's going on." I told him what had happened to us, that we needed a new car, and that we weren't in the mood for games. He understood. It turned out that his wife was a nurse in intensive care, so he understood tragedy. And he had seen us on TV. Most everyone had, and we were sick and tired of being recognized, since we're really private people.

He sold us the car without any sales tactics, and we were getting out of Dodge as fast as we could. We'd been driving since the day before. We'd stopped at a motel to sleep that night, and now we were getting close to the New Mexico border. There was farmland all around us with cows, bighorn sheep, and wild mountain goats grazing. At one point, I had to pull the car over and wait for about fifteen minutes for a herd of cows that had stopped in the middle of the road and didn't seem interested in moving. Beth and I watched them grazing, ambling along like they had all the time in the world.

That was exactly why we were heading to Jim's cabin in Colorado. We needed to stop time, stop the world, and take a break from everything and everyone. It seemed that disrupting events had started the day after we got home from the funeral when David Raemisch was formally charged with two counts of drunken vehicular manslaughter. He was let out of jail on $55,000 bail, and all the while, some of the people around us were making things harder for us. We knew they meant well, but some of them called to associate with us solely because we had been on television. That didn't work for us at all. Other people stayed away because they had no idea what to do or say around us, while still others were trying to be helpful, asking us what we needed. We had no idea. No one could make us feel better, and when they fussed about whether we were eating and sleeping enough, it drove us crazy.

A couple of weeks after the accident, I made two wooden crosses out of oak, and Beth and I pounded them into the ground at the accident site. People honked their horns as they drove by and called out things like, "Sorry for your loss!" On Jessica's birthday, we put up a sign at the site that said, "Honk for Jessica. She would have been ten today."

Just before we left for our retreat, we had to take the dogs to the vet. It was something minor for the dog, but when we told our vet we'd be gone for the next several weeks, she said, "Oh, it must be nice to be able to drop everything and just go away whenever you feel like it."

Beth began to cry, and she walked out of the room.

"You know what?" I said to the vet. "Sometimes you need to think about what you're saying before you say it. Our kids were killed two weeks ago, and we're trying to put our lives back together. That's why we're going away for a few weeks. It's not always what you think."

I tried to work during that time, but offering financial services to families to be prepared in case of a catastrophe had become much too painful. I remember being in our home office with Beth before we took off for Colorado. I was trying to sort through some paper work when the phone rang. I made an appointment for the next day and went to see someone. But when I got there and a potential client said, "I really don't need life insurance for my children," I didn't know how to deal with that. I realized that I couldn't keep doing my current job, but I didn't know what else I wanted to do.

On top of all of that, our lawyers were gathering evidence so they could reconstruct the accident site. It was all too much too soon with the lawyers, the district attorney, the sentencing, concerned friends and family, and my job all pulling at us. It seemed like everybody else's life was going on as usual while ours had fallen apart, so we took Jim up on his offer to get away.

"I want you guys to come to my little cottage in Colorado," he had said. "Come on up there, and stay as long as you want. I'll meet you there and get you settled in. It isn't much, but it's in the mountains. The air is fresh, and it's really private. I'm the last house on the road."

We were looking forward to some privacy as we kept winding uphill, watching the two-lane blacktop road turn into gravel. A river ran alongside the road for a while, and we passed a house or two with steeper hills ahead of us and a valley on the left-hand side. There were signs of age and wear on the houses, which were flanked by pine trees, scrub trees, and rock outcroppings.

We knew we were getting close when we stopped at a locked gate made from steel tubes that stood about five feet high. Jim had given us the combination to the lock. Beth got out of the car and punched in the numbers. The gate opened, I drove through, and after Beth closed the gate behind us, she got back into the car. We looked at each other with disbelief. It felt like we had just shut ourselves off from the world, which was exactly what we had in mind. We didn't want to answer the phone anymore, and we didn't want to turn on the television and see the same footage of the accident or see David Raemisch's face and hear what was happening with his case. His lawyers were trying to rally support for him, presenting him as a victim, and it turned our stomachs. We decided we would deal with all of that when we got back home. For now, we intended to disconnect from the world at large, connect with each other, and try to heal our broken hearts.

Beth

When Rick and I got back from the funeral, before we were scheduled to leave for Colorado, we started going to bookstores for some answers. We found plenty of books on grief, loss, and forgiveness, but very little about communicating with the dead. I found various books on angels, which I liked. I had always believed in them. We found a sweet tidbit here and there about how someone else had dealt with tragedy. I bought a few books, but I didn't find anything of substance about spirit communication. I was interested in a book about "automatic writing" and thought I might give it a try. You were supposed to think about your loved one, hold a pen loosely in your hand, and imagine that the words you spelled out were his or hers rather than your own. I tried it, but I wasn't convinced that the words I was writing were necessarily coming from anyone but me.

We even bought a Ouija board. We were willing to try anything, but nothing showed us a definitive way to communicate with the kids. It was all about gathering smatterings of information here and there. We packed the books we had been collecting to take up to the mountains with us, but I remember thinking that when we found a way to communicate with the kids, we would have to write our own book about it. Surely there were other people in the world who had gone through what we had gone through and were looking for answers like we were.

Sleeping was a problem for me, and although Rick slept better than I did, I kept waking him up in the middle of the night. I would toss and turn, look at Rick, and think that he had stopped breathing. I was terrified he would die too and leave me here all alone. I was just so troubled and filled with grief. When the people around us tried to be helpful by saying, "God only gives you as much as you can handle," it made me angry. Did that also mean that if I couldn't handle this, my kids would still be alive? I clearly couldn't handle the loss of my children, and I was pretty angry at God. I also got tired of hearing friends say, "You're so strong. You'll get through this."

I didn't feel a bit strong. I felt broken, but I had to get through it. What other choice did I have? I only realized how strong I was when I would visit the accident site in my brain, which was much too often. Each time I showed up there, I would tell the kids' spirits, "I'm sorry, I can't stay here for very long. It'll destroy me." I somehow knew that returning there over and over was like getting stuck in a loop; I needed to move on. That was where my strength came in, when I resisted getting stuck in a never-ending loop of pain and repetition, as I did what I could to tear myself away from watching the accident occur over and over. I realize now, when you experience something terrible once, and then you keep on going back and feeling it all over again, it's a classic sign of posttraumatic stress disorder (PTSD). It was close to impossible to stop. It was driving me crazy, so I did everything I could to get off the loop and get into the present moment.

A week before we left for Colorado, I remember asking Rick one morning, "Why am I taking these birth control pills? There's no control in this world, so why should I bother?"

I was ready to throw the pills into the trash, but Rick said, "Please wait. We need to heal from this before we decide whether we want another child."

"I'm f---ing never going to heal from this," I said. (I swore a lot during that period.) "But I'll keep taking the pills if you want me to." I took them for the rest of the week until I woke up one morning and told Rick, "I had a dream."

"I had a dream too," Rick said.

"But you never dream."

"I know."

The gist of the dream we had shared was the message that I needed to get the chemical out of my body. We both knew it was the birth control pills, so I threw them away, and we headed out about a week later.

We stayed over at a motel on the way, and I got a message from Josh in a dream. He told me that I would see a bright light in a door; that bright light would be him. Now I was even more anxious to get there. But when we stopped the next day for a bite at a family restaurant along the way, I got depressed watching people interacting with their kids. That had been us, a family of four, less than a month ago. Now, it all looked foreign to me. I wasn't normal anymore, and neither was my life. Nothing seemed to fit. I wasn't a mother anymore and when I saw a mother losing her temper with her child, I wanted to rush over there and remind her that her daughter was still alive. What did she have to be angry about? I'd have given anything to have my children with me, no matter what they were doing or how they were acting.

As we continued on the last leg of the trip, the river disappeared. We passed several stables and some grassland. I could hardly wait to see Jim. He had told us he had a few friends there who would be staying at his place, but they would be leaving in the morning. Jim was one of the few people who made me feel hopeful.

Jim was such a special man in our lives. He was the first person who had introduced me to the spirit world and to the possibility of connecting with my kids after they had died. He had become a lifeline, and I wanted to make sure I paid attention to each and every pearl of wisdom he offered me over the few days he would be there with us. I appreciated that he didn't preach at me or teach or try to make me believe anything. He didn't claim to be spiritual or all knowing. He didn't see himself that way, and he didn't have any theories about the accident and God or how I could cope. His connection to Spirit was simply a part of him, and he was so integrated, I wanted to be around him as much as possible in case I could get a tidbit about my children. I'd be satisfied with anything that he saw or felt.

On the way to our destination, each time Rick and I stopped to eat or to put gas in the car, I took out my journal and wrote things like, "Got to get to Jim's little cottage. Can't wait to see him. Just a few more hours." But when we pulled up to the supposed "little cottage," we were amazed at how large and beautiful it was. . We knew immediately that we didn't want to be anywhere else. This would be our sanctuary for the next few weeks. I breathed in the fresh mountain air. I was still in my private hell, but with the help of Kathy and Jim, I believed that my children's spirits were alive. I clung to these beliefs as hard as I could. Whenever I saw Jim, I was like a kid in a candy store, pleading with him, "Tell me more. What else did they say or do?"

Jim's cottage was actually a rustic, two-story house with a kitchen, dining area, and denlike room for reading and watching movies on the main floor. DVDs were popular at the time, but a shelf was filled with old VCR tapes. The bathroom and shower were in the basement, and the bedrooms were upstairs. The house was old and comfortable, and it got very dark at night with no ambient light from neighbors' houses or streetlights. When I woke up at night to go to the bathroom, I didn't want to be alone in the dark, so I woke up Rick, and together we made the trip downstairs to the bathroom and back up to the bedroom.

There was a covered front porch with rocking chairs. When you sat and rocked, you could see several outbuildings and a small stable, although there were no horses at the time. Jim's several hundred acres bordered the national forest, and a variety of footpaths led to trails that would take you up into the mountains.

The Colorado Sanctuary

When we headed toward the house for the first time, I was relieved that there were no kids playing outside. I couldn't have taken that, and when I saw Jim, I felt some hope come flooding in. That evening after Jim's other friends went to bed, Rick, Jim, and I sat on rocking chairs after dinner, talking about life and nature and bits and pieces of how Jim viewed the spiritual nature of things. He was a good conversationalist, and I could never get enough of what he had to say.

The next morning, his friends left, and he began to show us around. We learned to drive the six-wheeled gas-powered vehicles called Gators. There were three of them there, and we could use them to get higher up the mountain. Then we could get off and start our walks from there. The elevation was six thousand feet. The highest spot was ten thousand feet, and near the top, Jim told us, there was a waterfall and an Indian burial ground. In the backyard, hummingbirds flitted around the feeders Jim had placed there. On the first day, a hummingbird landed on my hand. They had no reason to mistrust human beings. As gentle as things were, though, Jim warned us to take a gun when we went on walks to ward off the bears. We were in the mountains, and there were wild animals around. We had to be aware.

Rick kept saying how beautiful everything was, and I agreed, but I couldn't really take in any beauty at that point. All I could do was look around me, breathe in the fresh air, and cry. That would have to be good enough for a while, I thought as we waved good-bye to Jim a few days later. He was going back to civilization, and we were staying alone in our sanctuary to breathe, cry, and connect with each other as we tried to make sense out of a life that no longer seemed to make any sense at all.

Beth and Rick in Colorado

9

Visitation

Beth

WHEN RICK AND I got married in 1987, I was working at a company called Curtis Mathis. My job was selling electronics, like TVs and VCRs. My boss, Brian, died in a car accident. He did a lot of traveling, and he fell asleep at the wheel on his way home one evening. Right after he died, I began having dreams about him. This was before we had kids, when I still had the luxury of being able to loll around in bed on the weekends.

While I woke and dozed during those yummy sleepy mornings, Brian and I would have conversations in my dreams. When I woke up, I remembered what we had said, and I told Rick I was worried that Brian was so prominent in my dreams. Maybe he was preparing me to die too. Rick didn't think that was the case, and shortly after that morning, I had another dream. All I saw was a white light, and I heard Brian's voice saying he didn't want to scare me, so he wouldn't be visiting me in my dreams anymore. I never saw him again until now.

Those dreams had been significant in my life—it was the first time I ever talked to a spirit or an angel. I'd had regular dreams all my life, where strange things happened and images shifted, but when I started dreaming about Brian, it was more than a dream. When I saw Brian in my dreams again after so long, this time in Colorado, I knew Jess and Josh had to be close. I asked him where my kids were. He said he would take me to them. I grabbed his hand. I was amazed I could touch someone in my dream. We headed toward a wall, and then we passed right through it. I went through another door, and I saw a circular clothing rack. When I pushed away the clothes, there were Jessica and Joshua, smiling at me. This was exactly what I had been looking for, a way to contact my children in the world of spirit.

I cupped their little faces, stroked their hair, and gave them kisses. I was so happy to be able to kiss them, to feel them, and to love them again. But then, without warning, everything went black, and I felt myself getting sucked back into the other world, as if I were traveling through a funnel at warp speed. It didn't scare me. It brought me peace. But I was disappointed that I had to leave. If I could have gone to that realm at will and stayed as long as I wanted to, I might not have come back, but I didn't seem to have that choice. I still don't. It's not set up for me to contact spirit. Rather it's spirit contacting me.

Colorado was a perfect place for spirit connection because the bedroom where Rick and I slept got very dark in the evenings since there were no city lights. The bedroom had a door with a window in it that led out to a porch. Late one night, I awoke to something unusual. A diffuse glow seemed to be pouring into the bedroom through a window in the door. I stared at it for a few minutes. I remembered my dream in the motel that first night when Josh had told me he would appear to us as a bright light when we were in Colorado. And there was the bright light. We hadn't left any artificial lights on, and the moon wasn't out. I couldn't imagine what else that light could be, so I woke up Rick. He was getting used to my waking him up to make sure he was breathing, but it was different this time. "Quickly. Look at that light," I said to him. "Josh is here. He said he would be a light in the window."

Rick saw the same diffuse glow that I did, and although this kind of thing was new to us, we both sensed that we were feeling the presence of spirits, that we were having a visitation. Jessie was somewhere else this time; I was pretty sure of that, and Rick agreed. But Josh was right there.

The next morning, when I woke up, I remembered I had dreamed of the kids.

Rick and I are in bed in Colorado, and the kids are spirits. They jump on Rick's and my stomachs so hard, we say, "Oomph." Then they begin to show us that they can take any shape they please, like Casper the friendly ghost, as they playfully give each other "noogies." I ask Josh if he's happy, and he says, "Yes, but I'm broke." Rick and I pull out some cash from our pockets and give it to Josh. He stuffs the money in his own pocket. Rick gives him more because he can't believe how cool this is. I'm surprised to see them as spirits.

During our time in Colorado, I hardly ever stopped thinking about the kids, and if I did, I felt badly about it. If I watched a two-hour movie and got lost in it and enjoyed it, when it was over, I realized I hadn't been thinking about Jessie and Josh for a while. I would have terrible guilt pangs. When I did anything for enjoyment back then, I felt guilty, and I sobbed.

Part of my problem was that I just couldn't stop replaying the accident in my mind, trying to figure out how to get the kids back, how to change what was unchangeable. I felt like the secret agent MacGyver, from the old TV series, refusing to take no for an answer while I was plotting a way to go back in time. I just didn't want to let go. I was a fixer at heart, and I believed with enough effort and stealth, I could fix anything—even the deaths of my children. I wanted to hang on to them. I was trying to find a way to get control of the situation, but clearly, it wasn't working. There was no way to control or change what had already happened, but I kept bargaining with God and doing everything I could to reverse that terrible Sunday afternoon, just in case.

During our month-long stay in Colorado, as we were trying to come out of the shock and grief that was running our lives, Rick and I did almost everything together. We didn't want to be out of each other's sight for an instant. We didn't want to be separated, which was strange because we had always been such independent people. But being together was a part of our healing, and if one of us saw unusual energies or movements in the house, if there was any sign that the kids were around, we both wanted to see them and feel them. We didn't want to miss anything, like the times when we were in bed and felt pressure on the mattress, as if Jessie and Josh were lying on the bed beside us. Sometimes we felt them lying across our bodies, and we didn't want to move so they would stay there as long as possible. We could feel other spirits around also. Rick said it felt as if a powerful spirit presence was holding us, incubating us, cradling us, and allowing us to heal and grow. For me, it felt like we were being born again, like a chick just coming out of its shell.

Rick

There were times when I was dropping off to sleep that I would tell Beth, "The kids are here. Somebody is resting on my arm." We were reconnecting with each other, and when we felt the kids with us, it felt like we were a family again. We spent a lot of time poring over our spiritual books, looking for ways to communicate with the children, and we hiked into the mountains almost every day. The air was clean and fresh, and we were getting close to nature, which was the kind of nurturing energy that we needed so much. We had successfully stopped the world, and I was melting into the beauty that was all around.

For me, it was a time of contemplation; I was working on accepting what had happened. I was an old hand at making lemonade out of lemons. You get like that when you're raised in an unpredictable alcoholic family, and I was trying to make sense of the hand we had just been dealt. I knew that acceptance was the only way to stop the pain. I had learned that the hard way during my childhood, and I was rerunning the accident. But while Beth was bargaining with God and trying to get the kids back, I was recognizing how much help had been there for us when we needed it.

When I fit the pieces together, I became more and more convinced that what had happened was meant to happen. I thought about the off-duty cop who suddenly showed up and was holding my head. I remembered the Flight for Life helicopter that was already in the air and the husband-and-wife doctor team who just happened to be at that intersection and had worked on Jessica. Then there was the fact that Beth and I survived the impact with almost no physical injuries. It was easy to imagine what might have happened if I had been two or three seconds earlier or later, if we had gone back home for Beth to change her shirt, or if we hadn't gone to the mall at all. But that isn't what happened.

Beth and I had done everything possible to keep our children safe. We taught them fire safety. We warned them to keep away from guns. We all stayed home on New Year's Eve to avoid drunk drivers. We bought a minivan to protect them from head-on collisions, and we always made sure their seat belts were fastened. What more could we have done? The more I thought about it, the more I had to acknowledge that we couldn't have changed what had happened. Everything was done that could be done, and during my time in Colorado, where I could think in the silence and sleep in the fresh air, it all started to make sense. It was during those quiet times when I came to believe deep in my heart that Spirit had been there. The accident had happened for a reason, and part of that reason was about us evolving spiritually.

I didn't share most of this with Beth, though. My acceptance of the events around the accident started out being unpopular with her. She was already annoyed that I was calmer and more at ease than she was, and I didn't want to rock the boat too much while she was trying to regain her footing. And so I refrained from telling her that we needed to be open to the invisible worlds that took up as much space as our tangible world did. I had a sense that was where our kids were. I wanted to figure out how to communicate with them, and so did Beth. I believed that in the bigger picture, embracing the invisible worlds was the only way to heal, but timing was everything.

Beth

I have to tell the truth; I was angry that Rick didn't seem to be suffering as much as I was. It's not that I wanted him to suffer. I love him, and I never want him to suffer. But I resented his speedy resolve that the accident was meant to happen.

"How can you accept it?" I said to him. "I'm still bargaining with God to get the kids back. It feels like you're giving up on them."

Part of my dilemma was that if I accepted the idea that the accident was meant to be, did that mean that David Raemisch didn't have to take responsibility? That he wasn't to blame because it was meant to be? To this day, I fear that when I say that the tragedy was meant to happen, that it was God's plan, it'll be like giving a free pass to drunk drivers, showing them a way to give up responsibility for causing a tragedy. The truth remains that if Mr. Raemisch had sat it out and not gotten into his car drunk, none of this would have happened. But it did happen. My children died; that was not OK. Rick and I finding a way to accept the unacceptable didn't diminish the terrible thing that someone did to us.

I could see that though Rick was finding a way to accept the accident while we were in Colorado, I wasn't. But as we talked about everything, I had to admit that the coincidences were astounding. And we were both benefiting from the clean air, the wonderful hikes, and the different times that we felt the kids close by. It was such a relief not to have to answer the phone, talk to family, or explain anything to anybody. I didn't have to watch parents interacting with their kids; I needed a break from that. Nobody was telling us what to do or checking up on us. We had no communication with the lawyers and only a little bit with the district attorney while we were away. They had started preparing our case when we left town, but nothing could happen until the sentencing. I'm happy to report that while I was having dreams about Rick and the kids and the spirit world, I didn't dream about the man who killed our children. I still haven't. He has stayed out of my dreams, and I intend to keep it that way. His part in the tragedy was and remains between him and God. It has absolutely nothing to do with Rick or me.

About two and a half weeks into our retreat, Rick got really sick for four days. One of those nights, I had a dream that Jessica was lying beside Rick in the bed. They were facing each other, with her arm around him. Rick recovered pretty quickly, thank goodness, and we continued to read, hike, sleep, and talk nonstop about what had happened and how to interpret it.

One day toward the end of our retreat, I was sitting on the porch when it occurred to me that my menstrual cycle was off. I'd been due to get my period the second week, but it hadn't come. I'd figured that the upset had thrown me off. I had thrown away my birth control pills after Rick and I had the same dream. We had been intimate, so we took a drive together down to the local pharmacy and bought a pregnancy test.

Sure enough, it was positive. I was absolutely stunned and ecstatic that God would give me another baby. I was going to be a mother again, and I knew this pregnancy was a gift straight from God. Rick was overjoyed too. He was going to be a father once more, and we both could focus on something positive. Even though we still had a lot of grieving to do, now we also had something to look forward to.

We decided to keep the news to ourselves for a while, especially when we flew Rick's mom up to Colorado at the end of our trip. She was having such a hard time. She was falling apart, and we thought maybe being in the clean air and being able to talk to us would help. She stayed with us for four or five days, and when we flew her back home, we made a vow that we were finished taking care of people. It was all too much, so we decided that rather than bring anyone else here to our sanctuary, we would stop in New Mexico and spend some time with my folks.

10

Shifting the Focus

Rick

IT WAS EARLY September 1999 when we left Colorado behind and headed back to the real world. We were sad to leave our mountain sanctuary where we had stopped the world. During our retreat, we had successfully kept the madness at bay for close to a month––no reporters hounding us, no TV stations airing our pictures every time Raemisch appeared in court, and no one recognizing us at the grocery store. We had time to walk, sleep, be together, and just think.

Now, we were on our way to Las Cruces, New Mexico, to spend time with Beth's parents. We stopped in the town of Taos to visit a psychic there. We had seen a few psychics on our way to Colorado, but they didn't offer us much. We understood that real psychics were few and far between. On the way to Las Cruces, however, we found a woman who seemed to be truly connected to Spirit. The moment we walked into her reading room and sat, the lights began to flicker on and off. It was Josh; we were all certain of that, and he sent us a beautiful message through her:

We never left you.

We are constantly in your presence. It will become clearer to the point you will not only hear us but see us and converse with us as if we are embodied. We will provide guidance for both you and the baby. Within three months, Mom, you will channel. Dad, you will first be healed and then heal others. The purpose of our death will be revealed. Live your lives to the fullest. We never left you.

It comforted us somewhat. We spent a few nights with Beth's parents, and then we returned home to get on with our lives. I tried going back to my job, but it was no use. I couldn't bear to try to sell life insurance and talk about death to families who were not open to taking out a policy on their children. I could hardly blame them, but I was much too raw, and I needed time to ground myself and prepare for the upcoming court proceedings. At this point, several things were happening at the same time.

Raemisch had been released from jail on $55,000 bail nearly a month earlier, on the day that we'd buried the children. He'd been charged with two counts of drunken manslaughter with the use of a vehicle,. Needless to say, it wasn't working, but they managed to keep him at home for Christmas and New Year's by asking for and receiving numerous delays and continuances. It hardly seemed fair. We didn't have the option of spending the holidays or any other times with our children.

We met with the DA almost immediately when we returned home, and he suggested that we start having a presence in the courtroom. So far, we had done no interviews with the media and made no appearances at court. Being photographed and publicly interviewed went against our natures. But the DA felt that if we began to show up in the courtroom when Raemisch appeared for hearings, the judge might feel connected to us and would be reminded of the impact that the accident had made. It was time to show the judge that we were real people and that our children had been real too. That would work in our favor when Raemisch was sentenced.

Starting in November, whenever he was required to appear in court, we showed up about an hour ahead of time and went to the DA's office in the courthouse. There, they told us what to expect that day. There was a group of associates there who worked with victims of crimes, acting as liaison between the attorneys and the victims, and they took us along a back route to the courtroom when it was time so we could avoid photographers and reporters. We would enter the courtroom and stay at the back to listen quietly to the proceedings. When it was over, they would take us back up to their office using the same back route and explain what had just happened. The media were still hounding us for statements and interviews, but we had no interest in the limelight. We made a conscious choice not to respond to any requests, and eventually, they began to leave us alone.

A little later in the process, however, we let one TV station into our home so they could get some pictures of the children. We wanted their faces out there, to show that we were a real family and to counteract the fact that Raemisch's attorneys were writing letters to the newspapers on a regular basis. "He needs help with his disease, alcoholism, not incarceration," they would say, as they tried to rally public support for zero jail time for this man who had blindly taken the lives of our two children.

In the meantime, we started searching for counselors for Beth. By the time we left Colorado, I had basically come to terms with the accident. I was still grieving—that would go on for a long time because I missed the kids so much—but I had spent the last month looking deeply into the events, and when I went over the details, I came away believing that Spirit was there and it was meant to happen. I was convinced it had happened for a reason, but Beth didn't agree with me yet. She got mad at me whenever I said that I was OK and told her that I believed Spirit was there. She thought that I was not honoring the children when I expressed my opinion that the accident was meant to be. We needed to find some help for her while we dealt with her secret pregnancy and all the legalities in front of us.

Beth

While we were away, our lawyers had been compiling evidence, reconstructing the accident scene, and building their case for the civil suit. They would have to prove to the court that Raemisch was guilty which would not be difficult. When you looked at the facts, there was one man driving drunk at eighty miles an hour and two innocent children with their seat belts fastened in a minivan stopped at an intersection. Really, there was no possibility of a trial; everyone knew he was guilty, and the insurance company didn't argue about it. Raemisch's father had an umbrella insurance policy on his car, the one that had been involved in the accident and had caused a great deal of damage and injury.

I finally had Rick convinced that we didn't need the contract that awarded one-third of our settlement to the lawyer. We called Fred. We knew him better than his partner, Rob, and agreed to a meeting at the local Dairy Queen. It was November 4, and we spoke for about an hour. In the end, Fred told us not to worry about the contract. "If your case doesn't go to trial, I'm sure Rob won't take a third." When Rick and I headed back home, we felt safe. Either way, we believed Fred was taking care of us, that he had our backs in this. Who would take advantage of us after all we had been through?

Even though we felt at ease about the lawsuit now, dealing with all of this was excruciating to both of us, so we appreciated a kind gesture by a neighbor. Josh loved football, and the Green Bay Packers were his favorites. A neighbor sent the team a letter and a newspaper clipping of what had happened to us, and they sent us a condolence card.

Despite the kindness of some of the people around us, I was drowning in sorrow. I knew I needed professional help, so we began to look for counselors to help me deal with my grief. Rick he went with me each time we interviewed a new counselor. Before we decided on someone we thought we could trust, we interviewed several counselors, and each was more inept and ridiculous than the last. During the first forty-five minutes of a session, I had to retell our tragic story and relive the scenario. Whenever I started to talk about my life and retell the story, it felt like it was happening all over again. *Haven't Rick and I been through enough?* I kept asking myself. To add insult to injury, we had to pay each of these people we ended up seeing, who all seemed like a bunch of crackpots.

All the counselors did was ask questions, not to be of help, but rather because they were curious about what had happened to us. One counselor told me I should scream and beat pillows to release my anger. Another one said that while she hadn't experienced this kind of loss, she had been plenty upset during her divorce, which made her qualified to help me through my pain. It seemed like no one could imagine or touch the level of pain I was experiencing, so after enduring meetings with a number of incompetent counselors, we settled on a woman named Ginny, who was nontraditional in her methods. She had incorporated shamanic healing into her practice, and she had been recommended by Katrina, Rick's sister, who had been seeing her for a while and liked her very much. It was helpful that she already knew about our family dynamic.

We were seeing Ginny weekly, and at first, she offered me what she called "memory regression," which had worked well with some of her clients. Apparently, it was a technique that would erase your memory so you didn't ever have to think about or feel the pain again. That might have been appropriate for other people, but it wasn't right for me. "I don't want to get rid of my memories. They're a part of me," I told her.

"Are you having nightmares?" she asked.

"No."

"Do you want some medication?"

"No."

I wanted to love, honor, and remember my children forever. But soon afterward, Ginny made a suggestion that Rick thought was appealing. She talked about energy healing and told us about a Cuban man, an

Inkan shaman, called Alberto Villoldo, who had taught her about sha-manic healing using stones and breathing exercises. Ginny was integrat-ing these techniques into her clinical practice to help her clients release stuck energy, and she thought we might be interested in attending one of his workshops. Rick liked the idea, and I was glad to have something to do. I couldn't just sit around the empty house all day, and the therapy with Ginny wasn't helping. The death of my children was so massive and out of the normal day-to-day experience, it seemed like it was not of this earth, so I was willing to look for help beyond the usual boundaries.

In mid-November, the sentencing had not happened yet, so we signed up for a weekend seminar with Alberto in Salt Lake City, Utah. It was mostly Rick who was interested, but I went along; I was still hang-ing on to his shirttails, and I didn't know what else to do. The workshop was scheduled for Friday afternoon and all day Saturday and Sunday. So after we signed up, we flew to Salt Lake City.

Rick

Beth and I continued to be frustrated by my family. Since they lived much closer to us than Beth's family, our interactions with them were more frequent. Their ideas of what we should be doing and how we should be helping them were different from ours. We lent them some money in an effort to be supportive, and we hoped it would help. In the meantime, we still had plenty of healing to do.

I was hoping that while Beth and I worked with Alberto to heal our-selves, maybe the rest of my family would get some healing, too. We were doing our best to stay connected to the family when Beth and I took off for Salt Lake City to explore something called "energy healing" that was being offered by a shaman named Alberto. Little did I know that the entire focus of my life was about to change, and I would welcome it with open arms.

11

The Medicine Wheel

Rick

SHORTLY AFTER WE landed at the airport in Salt Lake City, I spotted a short man with olive-colored skin walking through the terminal. He was wearing a cowboy hat, he had a slight limp in his gait, and he looked stressed out. A taller man walked behind him, maybe an attendant or an assistant, carrying five or six different-size suitcases and boxes. It looked like he was toting a heavy load, and I wondered if the shorter man was Alberto Villoldo with an aide carrying his things. But when we met him in person that evening, I was relieved to see that he couldn't have been more different. He turned out to be a calm, knowledgeable, and charismatic gentleman who inspired trust and ease in the people around him. The idea of someone else carrying his luggage seemed ludicrous after we spent some time with him.

About twenty-five of us were gathered in a large meeting room in Salt Lake City with no tables or chairs since Alberto followed the Inka traditions, one of which was sitting in a circle on the ground. I found out that Alberto offered two different types of training. One type, which was more advanced, was called the Light Body School, in which you learned to heal others. But since we were beginners, we were interested in the Medicine Wheel training, which encouraged self-healing. It had four parts to it: South, West, North, and East. Each direction focused on healing a different aspect of oneself. The workshop that we were attending was based on the south teachings, which were about shedding the past by releasing stuck energy.

When Alberto explained his shamanic philosophy, for some reason that I would discover later, it resonated with me immediately. He told us that according to shamanic teachings, everyone and everything is made up of energy. In fact, an energy body surrounds the entire physical body, to which all ailments can be traced. Disruptions in the energy field manifest outward into sickness and other kinds of mental and emotional disturbances. In order to heal, a shaman would identify those disturbances and trace them energetically back to the source of the original wounding. Once that was accomplished, the shaman would hold sacred space and work with his or her spirit helpers to clear the energy field, after which that disruptive energy would no longer manifest as ailments, unrest, or disease.

Born in Cuba, Alberto had been educated in Florida and California. He graduated from Saybrook University in 1969 with a bachelor's degree in Inter-American studies, followed by a master's degree and a doctorate in psychology in 1972. While he was on the faculty of San Francisco State University, he founded and directed the Biological Self-Regulation Laboratory, where he investigated the effects of energy healing on blood and brain chemistry. He did a great deal of research into the field of self-healing, becoming a medical anthropologist, working in a lab, and immersing himself in the Peruvian Inka teachings regarding the spirit/mind/body connection. During his research phase, he connected with shamans in Peru and became proficient in teaching these ancient Inka healing techniques.

Because the Inkas have strong ties to mountains and stones, when a student is studying either the Medicine Wheel or the Light Body training, he or she engages in what they call "building a mesa." This terminology means that a person creates an altar composed of sacred stones and a few other power objects. During the training, we were each instructed to look deeply within and come up with three events from the past that had made a profound impact on us. Then, with the use of three stones, we worked to heal those events. The previously stuck energy that got released was tied into that particular stone, and it became a part of this person's mesa.

I often travel with mine for healing and protection, and recently, when I went through security, one of the TSA agents looked at my hand luggage and remarked, "Look, he brought his rock collection." Between that comment and the sheer weight of the stones, I began to pack my mesa in my checked bag because carrying it was awkward, and I like having it with me wherever I go.

After Alberto had talked to us for a while and explained the foundation of what we were about to experience, he would introduce a particular technique, talk about the philosophy surrounding it, and demonstrate it with someone, and then we would choose a partner to try it with for ourselves. Before we chose our partners for the first exercise, I approached Alberto.

"I'm just curious," I said. "Do you want Beth and me to be partners?"

"Why do you ask?"

"We're here because we lost our two kids in a car accident, and we're trying to find ways to heal from it."

"When did it happen?"

"About five months ago."

He looked surprised. "No," he said, "I don't want you to work with each other."

"Beth is pregnant," I added.

Alberto picked a different instructor to work with both Beth and me, making sure it was someone who was advanced in the work because Beth was pregnant. But first he asked Beth if she felt comfortable allowing him to demonstrate an exercise with her. She agreed.

She lay down on the floor, and Alberto sat at her head, moving his hands in a circular motion to open what he called "sacred space" around her. Then he held his hands on the back of her neck, reminding her to breathe deeply. When he felt that she was completely relaxed, he identified a stuck *chakra*, a word that means "energy point" (there are seven chakras on our bodies), and opened it as he placed a stone on her heart chakra. He explained that the stone was helping to release stuck or dense energy, and we could see her arms begin to tremble. When Alberto sensed that the energy had been released through the chakra, he took off the stone and finished the exercise by moving his hands in a way that was meant to close that chakra and infuse healing energy into Beth's heart, which he said would jump-start the chakra once again.

As he performed the exercise on Beth, it was all new and fascinating to me. Yet, at the same time, it felt oddly familiar, as if I had always known about this kind of thing. In some cases, Alberto told us, the shaman performing the exercise would receive messages from the spirit world, which he or she would share with his or her partner. At times, the information might come from past generations. He was referring to a different world from the one in which we were living, the spirit world where we knew our kids were living. That was why we were there—to contact the kids in spirit and somehow communicate with them. I got the sense that this was completely right, that this was where Beth and I belonged, and there was a kind of relief in that. I had been concerned about Beth since the accident. I wanted her to get help, and it looked like we had finally found the right place and the right person.

Beth

I liked Alberto as soon as I met him. You could tell by his presence when he walked into the room that he had energy and power, but he never flaunted it. I liked his accent. He was kind and gentle. He had written a series of books based on his work, and since he was connected to the spirit world where my kids lived, I wanted to hear everything he had to say. I was really glad to be there so I could place my attention on something positive instead of replaying the accident in my head over and over. I was sick of it. I hadn't been able to stop obsessing over it, and

I really wanted to focus on learning something new. I needed to heal, and I sat there on the floor taking lots of notes at the beginning of the workshop, trying to grab onto anything that might make me feel better. It felt a little bit like being in school, and during a break, Rick let Alberto know that I was pregnant. We also told him about the accident. That was when he asked if he could demonstrate an exercise with me.

Before we began, he said, "Everything has energy. In Beth's case, she needs to release the impact of an accident from her body. Please lie down."

I lay down with my arms by my sides, and Alberto sat on the floor near the top of my head. I closed my eyes and breathed deeply for a while. I don't know how it happened, but my arms began to tremble and shake, and I felt as if something heavy and painful was leaving my body. It was a welcome release, and I felt safe and relieved to be in good hands that I could trust. What Alberto was doing made sense in the moment, and while we didn't tell everyone in the room the details of what had happened to us, Rick and I shared it with a few people who partnered with us during the weekend.

One of the nights I was there, I dreamed that I saw Jessica holding a door open for me. She said she was happy I was home, and when I woke up, I realized that our "home" was our new home in heaven.

Rick

Alberto began the class by talking about the energies of the South on the Inka Medicine Wheel. He described the Inka Medicine Wheel as an inner journey of healing, awakening and transformation. The Inka Medicine Wheel contains four directions and a person moves through the directions from South to West to North to East. The four directions represent different aspects of a person's physical, mental, emotional, and spiritual being. Each direction also represents a spiritual essence or energy. There are different healing techniques associated with each of the four directions as well. In each of the directions a person works to heal themselves, understand the spiritual energy of that direction and learn the healing techniques associated with that direction. He was referring to our energy bodies and the different things that might help people understand how those bodies function. He explained that we each needed to build our mesa with the help of three healing stones. When he told us that in order to be a healer, we had to heal ourselves first, I immediately recalled the message that Josh had sent us when we were in Taos:

"Dad, you will first heal yourself and then heal others."

One of Alberto's instructors, a woman named Linda, suggested that we imagine being held and protected in the arms of Mother Earth, a description that made a lot of sense to me. The material seriously resonated with me, and I could feel my stuck energy being released when I was practicing the exercise with my partner.

On Sunday, our last day there, Alberto told Beth and me that at the end of the session, he wanted to speak with us privately. After we had said our good-byes to the other people in the workshop, we sat down with Alberto.

"There are several things I want to tell you," he said, "but first of all, I want you to know that your children talked with me. When I was doing the healing on you, Beth, they were here. But to me, they look much different from how you view them. You see them as kids, the way they looked when they died. To me, they're strong, powerful spirits who have been around for a very long time. They were holding you and protecting you throughout the healing process, and they helped me work with you. They want to help you get through this pain."

Our hearts were touched by what he said, but it was odd to think about our children taking care of us and not the other way around. In fact, Beth and I were stunned and pretty excited as Alberto said, "Rick, you were knocked out during the accident, right?"

I nodded. "That's right." How could he know that? I hadn't told him. All we had said was that a drunk driver had broadsided our van and the kids were killed. We hadn't given him any other details.

"The reason you went unconscious," Alberto said, "is because you've been a shaman many times before this lifetime, and you helped the kids cross over. That was your role in the accident." Maybe that was how I knew that Josh had died before anyone told me. Alberto paused a moment and said, "The kids want you to continue to take my classes. I'd like that too. It's time for you to become a shaman again."

I was somewhat taken aback by that. A part of me felt like Alberto was giving me a sales pitch. It was pretty convenient for him to lure us into more classes and get more money from us. But a larger part of me reasoned that there was no way he could have known that I had lost consciousness during the accident. Beth had remained conscious, and he hadn't said that to her. He never gave off a sense of being a shyster or having ulterior motives. He seemed genuinely interested in both of us, and I trusted him because of how I felt with him.

When I really thought about it, all Beth and I wanted was a path to our children, a way to contact them. We had gone to bookstores over and over, at home and when we traveled, searching for anything we could find that might help us. We didn't need help with grief and loss. There were tons of books about that. We knew our children were still alive in the spirit world, and we were looking for ways to get into our children's world and communicate directly with them. We had visited counselors, we had talked to friends and family, and we had shelves full of books about angels and heaven that had cost us hundreds of dollars. We had kept on going back to the bookstores and buying more, but nothing had worked—until now.

At that point, I wasn't yet considering becoming a healer. Like Beth, I just wanted a path to the kids. This man was offering us one as he said, "I'd like you to come with me to Peru next month. We'll be visiting sacred sites, and we'll be there for the millennium. Y2K. Beth, you need to be able to see beauty again. Rick, you need to learn to become a healer. In Peru, I'll be offering more teachings from the Medicine Wheel. You both need to be a part of it. The kids want that for you."

I felt the truth in what he was saying. The trip to Peru was scheduled for the end of December. It was easy to imagine being in Machu

Picchu for the turn of the century. "We'll talk about it," I told Alberto, but I knew it was a done deal. Where else would we be rather be? Beth would be nearly five months pregnant, and it wouldn't do her any good to spend New Year's at home missing the children. Wouldn't it be better to be in a place where we could contact the kids and feel their presence?

When I looked over at Beth, I could see that, just like me, she was taken with Alberto and the things he had said. I could see a glint of hope in her eyes for the first time since the accident. She had perked up a little bit when Jim Phillip had talked about Josh and then again when she figured out what the chicken in the basket meant. But her reactions were nothing like the way she looked now. None of the counselors, including Ginny, had helped her at all. They had only made her more confused and frustrated. Now, she looked so different after this weekend, I could only imagine how much the trip to Peru might help her. And I was deeply attracted to this work, much to my amazement.

We flew home with images of Peru and contacting the children in our heads. I was grateful to Ginny that she had introduced us to Alberto. If that was all she gave us, then that was a lot. But when we finally told Ginny about our weekend, we had no idea she would turn out to be a catalyst for us in a most uncomfortable and unexpected way.

12

Life or Death?

Rick

I'M THE OLDEST sibling of four in my family. I have a younger sister Kris; a brother, Jeff; and Katrina is the youngest. Beth also has three siblings: her older brother, Steve; a sister Jeannie; and then Laurie. Beth is the baby. Her mom and dad are still happily married after fifty-six years. She had a loving childhood with very little angst, and she couldn't wait to have kids of her own. When she finally did, they were the heart and soul of our family. Beth and I made sure to raise them as healthy, happy kids, the same way she was raised.

It seems that my youngest sister, Katrina, had a really tough time growing up in the shadow of our alcoholic father. It was hard for all of us, but she apparently suffered a great deal of abuse in her early years. Several years before the accident, when she was old enough to go to college, she left home and immediately attracted an abusive relationship. She struggled both personally and financially and went back home to live with our mother. When she got there, she decided that having a child would be a good thing for her, so she became pregnant through artificial means. Maybe she had hoped to do things differently when she had the chance, but it turned out that her daughter had medical issues that brought their own brand of difficulty. She and her daughter ended up living in our mother's house. My mother supported both of them, and we gave them close to fifty thousand dollars over a few years.

When my mother's coffers were finally empty, Katrina started asking Beth and me directly for money for new tires, doctors' bills, and a host of other things. I wanted my sister to be able to finish school. I thought it might set her up for a future in which she could take care of herself and her daughter. In October 1999, three months after the accident, Beth and I loaned Katrina several thousand dollars. About a month later, she asked to borrow more money and promised to pay us back when she got her tax refund.

When she asked for more, we asked her, "Where did the three thousand dollars go?"

She never gave us a solid answer; she muttered something about car trouble and a few other problems. When we hung up the phone, she sounded offended that we had asked her how she had spent the money we had given her earlier. We were stunned at her arrogance and decided not to loan her any more money. What was the point? How soon would she ask us again? But that wasn't the end of it.

We bought some new furniture for our living room. I knew that Kris needed a couch, so instead of getting rid of ours, we decided to give it to her. She lived near Ginny in Milwaukee so one day before we left the house for a counseling session, we heaved the old couch into the back of the car and headed for Ginny's office. Once the session was over, we planned to drive to Kris's house and give her the couch.

Beth

This was the first time we were seeing Ginny after our weekend in Salt Lake City with Alberto. I was anxious to tell her all about it. She greeted us as usual, and we sat down and began to explain what had happened to us during the workshop.

I told her about the energy exercises we did and the way my arms had trembled when Alberto was demonstrating with me. "Sometime during the weekend," I told Ginny, "I finally began to realize that the accident might have happened for a reason. I'm not completely sure yet, I have a lot more thinking to do, but I started to find some acceptance."

I expected Ginny to be happy for me. She had referred us to Alberto, and as a result, I was beginning to find a way to live with what had happened. I hoped my work with her would be a continuation of that. But her reaction stunned both Rick and me.

"So," Ginny said, "you're good with your children dying? Great. Are you ready to help heal your sister Katrina now?"

Rick and I exchanged glances. We were stunned and speechless as she continued, "I need to talk to you about Katrina. You loaned her money, and now you're being judgmental. You're not allowed to question her. She needs help, and you need to help her."

Obviously Katrina had complained to Ginny about our asking her what she had done with the $3,000. Now Ginny was telling us that Rick and I were judging his sister, that we were upsetting her. We were supposed to give her as much money as she wanted, ask no questions, and then give her some more.

"Now that you're OK with the kids dying," Ginny repeated, "let's get to work on Katrina. You said you'd help her finish school. You need to give her some more money, get online, and find some additional funding for her. And when you loan her money, you don't get to ask what she did with it. Your father hurt your sister, and you have to help her heal." I have no idea what the three of us discussed for the rest of the session. I was so angry. I imagined that Ginny could lose her license for talking to us like that. I was really upset when we left and headed over to Kris's house to drop off the sofa. I was trying to get over what had just happened. There's a famous expression by Irish author and poet Oscar Wilde, "No good deed goes unpunished," and we were about to see how true that was.

We got the couch into Kris's living room. It looked great in there, and we sat down for a few minutes to chat before we headed home. We expected she might thank us for the gift, so we couldn't believe it when she said, "I need to say something about Katrina."

Oh no, not again. Kris was in on this, too? She continued, "You need to give Katrina more money, and you don't get to ask her how she plans to use it or how she used the money you already gave her. You're making her feel bad. She really doesn't need that kind of judgment right now."

Both Rick and I could hardly believe what we were hearing. We were being judgy? We got into the car, and normally, I would have been boiling mad as we began the hour-and-a-half drive back home. But instead, I felt totally defeated. I was still weak and lost from the deaths of our kids. It was a struggle to get through each day, and now it felt like we were being attacked by the people who were supposed to help us. I had no idea how to deal with these daily events on top of the loss of the kids. I had seen a glimmer of hope during my time with Alberto, but after today, it felt like that hope was gone. My brain was crowded with thoughts. It was making me crazy, and all I could hear were Ginny and Kris, telling us we were doing it wrong, and we were bad people for questioning Katrina.

What about us? We'd lost our kids four months earlier, and we had been generous enough to loan money to Rick's sister and to give Kris a couch. We were the ones who needed to heal, and for Ginny to assume that everything was fine and dandy for us after four months and one weekend workshop was ludicrous and insulting. She was a professional counselor. We were paying her to help me, and all she was doing was making me feel worse.

My head was bursting when I told Rick, "I can't stop the voices in my head. I keep hearing your sisters and Ginny telling me what we're doing wrong and how we're supposed to help them. But how can I help anybody else when I can't even help myself? We try to do good. It's our money, and we're trying to help. Now we're the bad ones. All these voices are in my head. They're really loud, and I can't make them stop. What am I supposed to do?"

I felt like I was going insane. My children were dead, I was still replaying the accident, and the voices in my head wouldn't stop fighting with each other. I was on a roller coaster of emotions. People were chattering in my brain, and I couldn't stop them. I simply couldn't control my mind. I was fighting with God, and all I could think about was wanting to die and be with my children. I wanted to leave this earth where the people who were supposed to help me were hurting me. It was much too painful. But how would I do it?

I turned to Rick and said, "I can't stop the voices in my head, and I want to die. I'm going to go for a long walk into a snowbank and freeze to death. I just can't do this anymore." I looked down at my wrists. "I don't know how people slit their wrists. They call it being weak, but I think it's strong. I can't go on. There's no off switch. God should have given me a little toggle switch, but I don't have one."

Rick exhaled deeply and was silent for a while. Finally, he said, "Beth, if that's what you have to do, if you need to leave this earth, I can't stop you. I don't really have that right. I don't want you to do it. We already lost the rest of our family. You and I are all that's left, and we're about to have a new baby. But if you can't be happy, and that's what you have to do, I would understand."

I looked at Rick. He really thought I might do it, and in essence, he was giving me permission. But when I got home, I got out of the car and thought about the snow. I could take off walking right now, find a deep snowbank, bury myself in it, and freeze to death—but I had to go to the bathroom, and I hated the cold. I went into the house, went to the bathroom, and picked up the phone to call my mother. I wanted her permission to take my life, but of course, she wouldn't give it to me.

"I gave you life," she said, "and I won't give you permission to die. We're Catholics, and we don't believe in suicide. You'll end up in purgatory. I'm going to pray hard every day that you find the inner strength to go on."

I was at my lowest point since the accident. I couldn't find a reason to go on. I was questioning all of my Catholic teachings, but this was where those teachings saved me. When I thought about my situation, I knew where Rick was. He was beside me. I knew where my kids were. They were in heaven with God, and although I couldn't see them or touch them, I had begun to find a way to communicate with them in spirit and in my dreams. All of that was clear. Now I was pregnant, and I believed in God. If I took my life, I might end up alone in purgatory, and I had no idea where that was. That felt scarier than waking up each day without my children. Would I be alone in purgatory? And if I killed myself, I'd be killing the baby I was carrying too. I'd be no better than Raemisch.

I went to bed that night knowing I couldn't commit suicide. It was out of the question. But I also couldn't stay where I was. Rick and I needed to get the hell out of there, away from counselors and Rick's family and lawyers and hearings and the endless chatter of the people around us.

The kids and I were in the car, driving to West Bend together, trying to decide where they should go and play. Should we go to Jessie's friend Trisha's house or Josh's friend Derek's house? None of us could remember Trisha's or Derek's phone number, and Josh really wanted to see his buddy, but we weren't sure how he would handle seeing that Josh and Jessie were still alive.

The kids decided to stay with me instead, so we all went to the beach. Josh even managed to find some swimming trunks, and when we got to the sand, we grabbed a couple of people around us to have a drumming ceremony.

My dreams about the kids sustained me all throughout my healing process, and that night, I was grateful to have spent time with them. The work with Alberto was bringing me closer to them, and I was grateful and anxious to go further with him.

Although we never worked with Ginny again, it turned out that years later, Rick saw her in an airport when they were both heading to a workshop that Alberto was giving. When they arrived at the workshop venue, they had a long talk, and Rick told her that what she had said and done was devastating to us, especially to me. She was mortified, as well she should have been, and she apologized, but it was too little, too late for me.

It seemed to Rick and I that Ginny had become so focused on helping Katrina that she had become blinded to the fact that we still needed help. We could only assume that she was viewing us as another tool to use in Katrina's recovery. As a result of the tunnel vision that she developed, she completely missed the fact that I wasn't OK with my kids dying.

Rick and I needed a fresh start, and the idea of waking up in Peru on the first day of the New Year was appealing. On top of the loneliness from losing our children so suddenly, there were weekly reminders from the DA and our attorneys that the sentencing was coming up in January 2000. I couldn't stand the idea that Raemisch was allowed to spend Christmas and New Year's with his family after he had destroyed ours. There was no getting away from the stress, and the voices in my brain were not quieting down, so we made up our minds to go to Peru with Alberto for the turn of the century. We were getting out of Dodge, but there was a lot of resistance from family and friends. There was so much unfounded fear and confusion surrounding the millennium, the infamous Y2K; everyone thought we were in danger, and they tried to talk us out of flying anywhere.

My mother was adamant that we were making a huge mistake. She said, "You can't travel because you're pregnant." I was just starting to show, and she was afraid that being pregnant in a third-world country was dangerous and an unnecessary risk. The truth was that I was in more danger if we *didn't* go because of my uncontrollable thoughts. Rick and I both knew that a break was not only desirable; it was necessary. We had made up our minds. Some of our friends suggested that Alberto was taking advantage of us. "You're nuts," one of them said. "You can't go. This guy is a charlatan, and he wants your money."

That didn't ring true for Rick or me. Alberto had already helped us more than anyone so far, and we had only been with him for two and a half days. So although we had somehow gotten through Thanksgiving, the pressure was mounting from everyone around us, and we couldn't face New Year's at home without Josh and Jessie. We knew Rick's family would drive us crazy. They had already started, so we packed our suitcases and got ready to leave on our upcoming expedition a few days after Christmas.

We spent Christmas with Rick's family and made a separate trip to spend time with my good friend Sue and her family. I gave her daughters American Girl dolls, and they were delighted. Of course, it was bittersweet for me. I enjoyed their surprise and happiness when they opened their dolls. But unfortunately, I could only imagine Jessica having the same reaction, opening all those presents I'd bought for her six months earlier. I bought another Josefina doll, like the one we had buried with the kids, and I put that doll and Jessica's Kirsten doll away. If I had a girl, I would give the dolls to her. If not, I wanted to keep them anyway, so I found a safe place for them. My heart was somewhere else, but the idea of leaving the country after Christmas and communing with the spirit world where my kids were living kept me going.

13

Embracing the Unseen

Rick

IN THE PERIOD leading up to Christmas, we met with the attorneys a few times before our upcoming expedition to Peru. We had been showing up at court every few weeks for Raemisch's appearances, and Beth hid her growing belly under bulky sweaters so the defense attorney wouldn't have added ammunition to try to prove that we were fine and were getting on with our lives.

We weren't fine. We were far from it. I missed my children more than I can possibly describe, but I was making a perceptual shift, leaving behind the mind-set that I had lost them and they were gone forever. I realized that that kind of negative mind-set can only bring about more suffering. Instead, I became focused on connecting to Spirit and giving up the perception of loss about who our children might have become. I had stopped grieving that particular idea because I understood that you can't grieve something that would never exist. If the accident was meant to happen, it also meant that our kids were only going to be alive on this earth until the day of the accident. Accepting that stopped me from imagining a future that was not possible.

As my perception shifted, I was feeling more whole. I understood that in order to heal, I would need to open up and embrace the unseen and invisible worlds that most certainly exist. I was starting to sense that they took up as much space as—if not more than—our regular world did, and I had a reason to join that world because my children were living there.

Beth was still terribly distraught, but she was starting to embrace the invisible world like I was. Thank God she had made a commitment to stay on this earth and have the new baby. Now I hoped that our trip to Peru would help both of us, especially her, to heal our broken hearts. All we wanted was to leave the familiar world behind and create an enduring communication with our children. I had a lot of hope because we were about to spend some extended time with people who recognized the spirit world as being real and reachable.

We had two visits from attorneys during the weeks before Christmas, and so did Raemisch—one from our camp and one from the defense side. They came to talk with us and put together what they called an "impact statement." This was a declaration based on their visits to our homes as to how the death of our children was affecting our ongoing lives. Our attorneys told us that that the difference between Raemisch's home and ours was drastic and palpable. While his home was filled with sparkly decorations, colored lights, wrapped gifts, children, and a Christmas tree, our home had no Christmas decorations whatsoever, and there were no children running around. Instead of a tree, gifts, lights, and tinsel, we had taken pictures of the kids, framed them, and put them up all over the walls. We didn't do it for show. We did it for ourselves. We just didn't have the heart to celebrate Christmas without our kids, and we wanted nothing more than to find a way to feel them around us.

Beth

When Christmas was finally over, we breathed more easily. The Olsen Bank was officially closed for the New Year when it came to family. We were done with loaning money and with counselors. I just felt so betrayed by Ginny and by Rick's family. And some of our friends were starting to look at us as if we were weird when we talked about the spirit world.

We were packed and ready to go to South America. Our families were very upset that we were on our way to Peru for the turn of the century while I was pregnant. They were pressuring us to listen to reason, to stay home, while everyone chattered away about Y2K, expecting computers to stop dead at midnight and put everyone in danger. An airplane trip anywhere was not safe, they told us. It was pretty clear that our new way of thinking was way out of most of our friends' comfort zones, but the more they tried to convince us to stay, the more we wanted to go. We couldn't wait to be surrounded with people, most of whom were strangers to us, who regarded communication with the spirit world as normal and reasonable. We wanted to be with people who thought like we did and weren't afraid of journeying into the unknown and the unseen.

However, not everyone was dragging us down. I had several friends who listened and encouraged us. A neighbor was very kind and sensitive; she left little things on our porch like coffee in a cup with a muffin or some hand lotion. Her husband shoveled our driveway without asking us. There were some great acts of kindness, but when our plane finally took off and we left our familiar world behind, all I felt was relief. Even though I was four and a half months pregnant, I would do anything to get closer to my children, which was about to include numerous plane and bus trips, hiking mountains, and performing spiritual ceremonies in the middle of the night in the dark of the desert. We had never been to a third-world country before. However, when we finally landed in Lima, where we would spend our first night, whatever it turned out to be, I knew it could be no worse than what we were leaving.

Rick

We had a short stopover in Florida, and when we landed in Lima, I felt great anticipation. The area immediately surrounding the airport was seedy and run-down, which troubled me. But when we got to the hotel, we were in much nicer surroundings.

There were about eighteen of us who gathered at our lovely four-star hotel that first night to meet each other, have dinner, and a get good night's sleep before we flew the next day to Cuzco, where the actual expedition would begin. Cuzco is a small city in southeast Peru near the Urubamba Valley of the Andes mountain range. Our hotel there was much more rudimentary than the one in Lima. We had expected that. The room had a basic double bed and a ceramic-tile floor, and the shower had an electric heater that was installed right on top of the shower head. It looked like an accident waiting to happen, and it was. One night, it caught fire, and we had to leave our room while they extinguished it. We took it in our stride. We weren't there on a luxury trip or a vacation, and the hotel was comfortable and good enough for our purposes.

We spent the day in Cuzco getting acclimated and touring the city, which has ornate churches and examples of Inka-built walls that after so many years are still intact and functional. One day later, we boarded a train and then a bus that took us up the winding roads to Machu Picchu, an ancient city on a magnificent mountain ridge above the Sacred Valley through which the Urubamba River flows.

Once we were there, we cleansed ourselves in a short ritual before we hiked for about thirty minutes to reach some ancient ruins. We toured Machu Picchu until late. Then we participated in a ceremony with our Peruvian guides, which included some Q'ero shamans, direct descendants of the Inkas. There are a great number of myths and beliefs around the Q'ero shamans, including that they don't exist. But the ones with whom we traveled would disagree. They are a highly spiritual race of people who do not adhere to any dogmatic religious beliefs. Rather, they are mystical and flexible as they worship the Cosmic Mother, which includes the entire universe and Mother Nature. I resonated with their beliefs, which were quite similar to my own, although I could never have articulated them before I met them.

Ceremony in Machu Picchu

The next day, we traveled to a small town called Pisac by bus, where we did more ceremonies and visited another Inka ruin. There, we made *despachos*, offerings to the spirits for the healing of Mother Earth, which contained a variety of the following: sugar, incense, threads of gold and silver, and white flower petals. Each item was carefully and intentionally placed on a large sheet of white paper and arranged in the shape of a mandala. We added sacred fresh coca leaves, and then we blew our prayers into small bunches of leaves, which were added to the offering.

Beth

On the train to Machu Picchu, I had to go to the bathroom pretty often because I was pregnant. But when I looked inside the bowl, I could see the track beneath me as the train went rushing along. A small square of toilet paper cost a quarter. I didn't like that very much, but I would have done literally anything to get closer to my kids. And so, I hiked all over Peru while I was nearly five months pregnant. Things got scary sometimes, but I kept thinking that if the worst thing happened, and I slipped or had any kind of accident, I'd end up with Jessie and Josh. I knew they were hovering; I could feel them, and so could Rick.

At some point in the journey, Rick and I sat down for a session with a shaman who could read the coca leaves. He didn't speak English, but he told us through an interpreter that he sensed Jessie and Josh around us. I was stunned when his interpreter told us, "Oh, you suffered a loss."

"Yes," I said. "We had two kids who were killed. But how does he know that?" I asked the interpreter.

"It's right there in the coca leaves," he said and chuckled as if reading coca leaves was the most natural thing in the world. For them, it was. I also had a special moment in a place called Ollantaytambo, where Alberto suggested I sit on a rock that was just outside the ruins. Rick and I had hiked up the mountain, and we were two of the first people to reach the top. When the rest of the group caught up, there I was, perched on a rock that was traditionally used for honoring Mother Earth. Alberto told me to pull the energy into myself through the rock. It would be good for the baby.

Beth on the Pachamama stone

It was gratifying to be part of a group of people who regarded the spirit world with the same degree of acceptance that they displayed about anything else. This was the support we'd been looking for, the kind of support we couldn't get from books or people back home who had no idea what we were feeling and experiencing.

Rick

It was really sweet to watch Beth sitting on that rock while people in the group came up to her and just stared. It felt like she was supposed to be there, that she had always been there, sitting on that rock that was also an altar. Some of our group couldn't believe that she was on the expedition, nearly five months pregnant, moving up and down the hills with apparent ease, while some people were having a hard time getting up the mountains.

We savored the hiking and the ruins in the daytime. But on New Year's Eve in Machu Picchu, when the sun began to go down, Beth and I had a very tough night. It wasn't so much the dreaded Y2K, which had no particular meaning for either Beth or me. I was glad we hadn't succumbed to pressure from family and friends to forego this trip, but Beth and I both agree that the New Year was the low point of our trip. We ate dinner with the group, but when they started to become joyful and celebrate, we had no joy in our hearts, and we needed to be alone. We looked at each other and said, "What are we doing here? We have to get out of here. This kind of celebration isn't for us."

We left the dining room hand in hand and walked toward our hotel room, feeling Spirit presence everywhere. When we had first met Alberto in Salt Lake City, that had been our introduction to the Inka beliefs about the spirit world. Now, our time in Peru was our immersion into that world, which wasn't easy. In fact, it was so painful that it felt like we were being reborn, emerging from the womb as spiritual beings so we could find a tangible connection to Jessie and Josh.

As we got closer to the hotel, which was located at the base of the sacred mountain, I felt the spirits of not only our children but many others as well. It was the first time I had felt that kind of presence, which was more like a pressure. The night was pitch-black. There were no artificial lights along the path, and I felt an intensity that is almost impossible to describe. It felt like something was pressing in on us. I think it was a combination of energy from the sacred site, from the spirits who surrounded us, and from the people who were celebrating the New Year. It felt like I was walking through molasses; there was just so much energy, and it was so dense.

Later, both Alberto and a psychic from North Carolina who was traveling with us told us that they had seen our kids walking with us everywhere. She said, "I want you to know that your kids are always following you around. They're helping you. They're protecting you."

It was odd to think about our children protecting us since we had always protected them. But what Alberto and the psychic saw were strong and powerful spirits, eight or nine feet tall. The kids would always live in our memories as children, but I could also accept them as powerful spirit beings who walked beside us wherever we went.

On that night, the last of the old millennium, we were so overwhelmed with sadness, we went into our hotel room, climbed into bed, and wept. We were in a country where there were very few computers and rudimentary electricity and other utilities, so there was no fear of blackouts or any other kinds of technical problems. The trouble was that we were starting a new year without our children, and we were inconsolable. We fell asleep early, way before midnight, wondering what the new year would bring and how we would ever get through the pain and suffering.

Beth

We got up on January 1, got onto a chartered plane with the rest of our group, and flew to a place called Nazca, where our next hotel was located right on the ocean. After we checked in, we traveled by boat to a group of islands off the coast that were part of a nature preserve, a breeding place for sea lions, walruses, and seals. It was by far the most inspiring place we had seen as yet. We were about to walk among a series of ancient geoglyphs created somewhere between AD 400 and 650. We studied hundreds of individual figures that ranged in complexity from simple lines and curves to stylized hummingbirds, spiders, monkeys, fish, sharks, orcas, and lizards.

Nothing could outshine the walruses and seals, though. There were thousands of them, swimming, mating, and resting in the sun. Back in Salt Lake City, when we first met Alberto, he had given me a homework assignment: to find beauty. As lovely as the surroundings had been in Colorado during our retreat, I knew that there was beauty around me, but I couldn't feel it or take it in. I thought that once my children had died, I would never be able to appreciate anything ever again. I still felt that way when we landed in Peru, during the ceremonies, and while exploring the ruins. Then, on that boat in Nazca, in the midst of that breeding area with thousands of seals, walruses, and dolphins, I heard myself say, "Oh, this is so beautiful!" In fact, it was out of my mouth before I knew it. I had done it. I had found beauty when I wasn't even looking for it.

Beauty in Peru

From that moment on, the world looked different to me. I was seeing the splendor of nature, untouched and pure. The water was as warm as bathwater, the animals were magnificent, and although I still had a struggle ahead of me to hold on to a sense of wonder about the world, I had achieved my immediate goal. For however long it lasted, I had been successful at seeing beauty, and I would build on that, even though it would take some time for me to learn to hold on to it.

Rick

We spent several days in Nazca where we did a powerful ceremony along what they call the Nazca Lines in the middle of the night. Normally, people are not allowed to be there in the dark of night, but because of Alberto's connections, we were granted permission. There are huge glyphs drawn in the ground in Nazca, a desert area, and unless you flew over them, you couldn't see their complete shape. How they came to be there is somewhat of a mystery, but we didn't need to know as we began a walking ceremony.

There was a double spiral on the ground that looked like a large jelly roll when seen from the sky. Now, we were directed to begin walking along the outside of what was similar to a labyrinth that flowed inward. The idea was that as we walked farther and farther in, we were to imagine shedding our past, our history, and leaving it all behind. When we reached the center, it made a loop, and then we continued along a path that ran parallel to the first one as we walked back out.

I felt the presence of spirits so strongly, it took my breath away. Before we began, Alberto warned us, "Sometimes you have to be careful with what you're doing down here. If you step off the path, you can cause more harm to yourself than anything else."

I understood what he was talking about, as I could literally feel old energies dropping off me. I was wearing a black poncho that, from a shamanic standpoint, was meant to protect the body from negative energies. It felt like chunks of the past were peeling away from me as I kept on walking my way through it. When I finally got to the loop and began to walk back out, I was aware of what I can only describe as ghost figures, some of them related to the accident, some of them to my family issues, that had detached from my spirit and peeled away.

When we were finished with the ceremony and we had gathered around before heading back to the hotel, someone looked at me and said, "Rick, when did your hair turn white?" Apparently, the moonlight was reflecting on my head, and my hair was snow white. When I woke up in the morning, Beth and I looked at my head in the mirror.

"You were gray before, but your hair is white now."

It was more than the moonlight. It had actually changed color, and all I could do was shake my head. We were dipping into spirituality at a level so deep, there was no way to explain anything, so we didn't bother trying. We felt the kids around us countless times on the expedition, which gave us hope.

Our trip back home was shaky and unpredictable. Our plane was late, we missed a connection, and it took much too long. All we wanted was to get home and be able to climb into our own bed—and to enjoy the luxuries of first-world plumbing—but we felt satisfied because we had achieved our goal, and it all felt so right.

When we finally landed at the airport and went to retrieve our luggage, I knew I was not finished with Alberto and neither was Beth. He offered ongoing programs for each of the four directions on the Medicine Wheel, and he also offered the Light Body work in which a person could learn to heal not only him- or herself but others as well. I knew I would continue working with him. It seemed to fit me like a glove.

Most of all, however, I was deeply grateful for what had happened with Beth. She was like a changed woman. She had recognized beauty. She had also found some joy that had previously escaped her, and she was able to look at the future with hope and anticipation. We had both shed so much pain and sorrow that from then on, we were able to discuss the accident without becoming basket cases. No counselors or other healers were able to give us a gift like that. We had found what we were looking for, and we had only just begun.

14

The Sentencing

Rick

BEFORE WE'D LEFT for Peru in December, we suggested to our attorneys that we put together a short video for the sentencing, which was scheduled for the end of January 2000. The idea was to make the kids come alive for the judge, so we gathered together some VCR footage of the kids along with some still shots. At Beth's insistence, we also gave them some music for the background that added a personal and intimate touch to the five-minute piece. Once we had delivered the materials to the lawyers, we left the making of the video in their hands and set out for Peru.

It was only a day or two after we had gotten home when we went to the attorney's office to view the video. Out of respect for us, the attorneys started the tape and left the room, leaving us two large Kleenex boxes. They expected we would fall apart when we saw what they had done, but we didn't. When they walked back into the room and we weren't weeping, they were puzzled. It was partly because Beth wouldn't allow anyone to see her fall apart. But it was also because of our trip and the fact that we had communicated with Jessie and Josh all along the way. We were beginning to put things into a context we could live with. We had gathered courage on the trip, and we told the attorneys that they had done a great job with the video.

Our jet lag was still fresh when it was time for us to make some very important decisions. The sentencing was around the corner. It was scheduled for January 26, 2000, and we had to choose a number of family and friends, four people, to stand up and tell the court how they had seen the accident affecting us. Our hope was to have Raemisch incarcerated for as long as possible, but his attorneys were pushing hard for zero jail time. They had been very busy while we were gone, giving lots of interviews to the press, painting their client as a victim of a terrible disease, alcoholism. They weren't denying that his actions had caused our children's deaths. But they were calling him a loving father and a family man, and they insisted he needed treatment, not imprisonment.

We disagreed. It wasn't about revenge or rage. We never made him out to be a devil. We refused to give him that much power, and we ignored him as much as possible. But we wanted to see him in jail because as long as he walked the streets and had access to a vehicle, legally or illegally, no one on the road was safe.

As the date got closer, we chose people to speak for us who represented different aspects of our lives. Besides Beth's and my statements, which we would read at the end, just before they showed the video, we chose her brother, Steve; my longtime friend Neal; my mom; and the vice president from the insurance company where I had worked. These people had all weathered the storm of loss with us along the way and were picked to represent different aspects of our lives with Jess and Josh.

For several months, we had shown up whenever Raemisch was in court, deliberately making a presence in the courtroom so this judge would be aware that we were real people, and so were our children. The DA and associates were familiar with the judge who was presiding over the proceedings. They liked him; they thought he was fair, unbiased, and compassionate, which was why there had been so many continuances.

The defendant's side had stretched it out as much as they could get away with. Now we were tired of it all. This man had consumed so much of our energy since the accident; we were relieved that there would be no more delays because the other side had used up all of their allotted continuances. Beth and I were both anxious to get this behind us and see this man off the streets and behind bars where he belonged. We wanted our lives back. We were expecting a baby in three months, and this would put a period at the end of a sentence—Raemisch's sentence.

Beth

I pulled on a long, thick sweater to cover my pregnant belly. My family knew about the baby, but no one else did. I was in my sixth month. I couldn't hide it for much longer, and I was grateful I wouldn't have to. I was sick and tired of radio, TV, and newspaper journalists hounding us for interviews and photographs. We were tired of saying no. Now, it was finally the day of the sentencing, and by five o'clock, all of this would be over. It was almost surreal to get into the car that morning and head for the courthouse; we had been anticipating this day for so long.

We arrived an hour early, and we went to the DA's office, where we met with the people who would be standing up for us with their impact statements. The DA explained to all of us what to expect and how it would unfold to make sure everyone was on the same page. Then, when it was time, they took us along the back stairways to avoid the press, and we entered the courtroom.

Raemisch was already there, sitting with his lawyers. We had seen him on and off when we showed up for his hearings, and we had seen his picture in various newspaper articles. But this was the first time he would be seeing us, since we had stayed in the back of the room until now. Somewhere along the way, his lawyers had contacted ours to tell us that he wanted to send a letter of apology to us, but we were not interested. What good would it do? The kids were gone, and nothing he could say would bring them back. Did he expect us to forgive him? I could only imagine the excuses the letter would contain, and we left him on his own to figure this out with God. I still wasn't talking to Him.

In his opening remarks, the judge talked about the third car that had been involved in the accident. "We want to make sure that everybody has equal representation here," he said. He wanted people to remember that this man had suffered broken bones, that he was a victim too, and he should also be taken into consideration. He had chosen not to attend the sentencing because he didn't want to take the attention off our children's deaths. We appreciated that, but he also was affected by the drunk driver, and we agreed that he should not be forgotten.

The judge told everyone that this was the most difficult sentencing he had ever presided over, partly because of the deaths of our children and also because there was such an outpouring from the community. The judge had gotten literally hundreds of letters from both sides, and he assured us that he had read them all. He added that the impact of the accident was going to be decided not only by what had happened but also by what would happen going forward. He wanted Raemisch's people to understand that.

Prior to this, nothing had occurred in the Madison area involving drunk driving that suggested the possibility of such a long sentence, since the maximum sentence for two manslaughter deaths was eighty years, forty years a piece. This crime had not been premeditated, so we were aware that there was no way he would get the maximum, even though the DA was asking for it. Raemisch had been charged with two counts of involuntary manslaughter, drunk driving, and speeding. But these were the criminal proceedings, and along with jail time, we were asking for damages in the form of reimbursement for the children's funeral and the headstone.

After our four chosen representatives had told the court how they had seen the accident affect us emotionally, mentally, and financially, it was my turn to speak. Between loads of people from both sides and throngs of press and cameras, it was standing room only in the courtroom when I got up. But the room was dead silent. It was as if everyone was holding his or her breath, waiting for Rick and me to give our statements. I spoke off the cuff. I don't remember exactly what I said. I had written nothing down, but Rick had prepared a statement that was pretty eloquent.

Rick

Here are some excerpts from my impact statement:

> Your Honor, from the people who are here and the quality of the letters that you have received, I think that you are beginning to get a sense of who these children were. These were some exceptional children. My wife and I would often marvel at the comments we got from people regarding our children. We were proud of our children. We enjoyed our children. We talked with them often…We would talk about their day in school, what they learned, who they talked to, what they liked and disliked.
>
> We loved playing together as a family. There were many times when Beth and I would be awakened on a Saturday morning to the sounds of dishes rattling in the kitchen. Moments later our bedroom door would burst open with two smiling faces carrying breakfast in bed for Mom and Dad: cold toast, yogurt, and hard-boiled eggs. The breakfast would soon turn into a family wrestling match with giggles and laughter as Jess and Josh would try to help Mom tickle Daddy's feet.

I went on to describe our trip to the mall, the accident, and then what happened in the hospital.

> Beth and I walked hand in hand into a trauma room where they had been working on Jessie. I remember looking at all of that equipment in the room with those stark, bright lights. On a table in the middle of it all was my little girl. There was a tube sticking out of her mouth. Her face was an ashen color because she had lost so much blood. I touched her hand to say good-bye, and it

was already cold. I never did say good-bye to Josh. The next time I saw my children was several days later as they lay next to each other in their coffin. We buried them together, as they were always together.

I finished my statement with:

As my wife and I woke up the next morning, she asked me, "How do we go on?" That has been the question that we have been struggling with ever since that day. I have watched my beautiful wife turn into a shell of the person she was before. She was a full-time mom. She lived to take care of our kids. Her eyes used to sparkle every time she spoke of the children. When I look into those eyes now, I see despair. She has no purpose, no zest for life. It is a struggle just to get her out of bed every morning. She used to love cooking dinners for the family. She has cooked three times since July. She talks about leaving and suicide, so that she can be with her kids. Those kids were my best friends, she would tell me.

Somebody said that Mr. Raemisch shouldn't serve a long sentence, because he has suffered enough. He has to live with himself for what he has done. Living with himself is nothing compared to the suffering that my family has gone through and continues to go through. How can the suffering and pain that I see in Beth's eyes compare to that? How can his suffering compare to the mornings Beth and I lie in bed willing our bedroom door to burst open just one more time, longing to see those smiling faces, happy to be bringing us breakfast again. Beth and I will suffer for the rest of our lives.

When they showed the five-minute video right after my statement, every single person in that room cried. I'm not sure how long the whole thing took. It had lasted for three to four hours without a break when the other side was ready to present their statements.

Beth

The pain and sorrow in that room was indescribable. I wanted it to be over, and then I was blindsided when Raemisch's attorneys spoke. When I heard the form of punishment they were suggesting, it made my blood boil. First, they wanted their client to put on a suit and tie, not an orange jumpsuit, and talk to schools and groups about drunk driving. If that wasn't bad enough, they had the audacity to suggest that on Jessie's and Josh's birthdays and on the anniversary of their death, Raemisch should be required go to the cemetery and visit my children's grave.

I needed to stand up and say something right away. I asked my attorney to get permission, and the judge allowed it. "That is not going to happen," I said. "I don't want that man anywhere near the grave of my children. That's our sanctuary. I don't want to worry about seeing the man there who murdered my children when I go to be with them on their birthdays. That would be a punishment for me and my family, not for him."

When I sat back down, the judge was ready to give the sentence. He took some time to set the stage, going back over the facts. He reminded Raemisch, "You were out of control, and you broke the law. The fact is that you drove drunk and killed two children."

The judge cautioned the media to be respectful, not to get out of hand, and he announced his decision. Raemisch was being sentenced to twenty years for each child; the sentences would be served concurrently. That meant he would serve twenty years in all, probably a few years less for good behavior. He also told Raemisch that he couldn't write a book about the crime and that from now on, he could never use our names again in public.

There were outcries from both sides. Our people thought he was getting off easy, that twenty years was hardly enough. The other side thought it was far too much. I was no longer naïve. As for me, I'd known he would never get eighty years. Twenty would do, and it was satisfying to watch him being handcuffed and led out of the courtroom. Some of our friends and family were upset by the sentence, but all I recall is feeling relief—that it was over, that I didn't have to hide my pregnancy anymore, and that a drunk driver was off the streets. Maybe we could start to live again.

Rick

When the sentence was announced, the press rushed us, trying to get a statement. We didn't say a word as the DA escorted Beth and me and our families out of the courtroom and into the elevator. At the last second, just when the doors were about to close, a reporter managed to slide into the elevator, and he pushed a mic in my face. I said, "No comment," as Beth's brother, who stood six four and used to play football in college, grabbed the guy by his lapels and shoved him out of the elevator. Staying true to ourselves, we refused all interviews and denied press requests for copies of the DVD that had been shown in court. They had filmed it in the courtroom, and they would have to make do with what they had.

Over the course of the next several weeks, Beth and I were on TV all the time as the press showed clips of the sentencing, the longest sentence for drunk driving that Madison had ever seen. We saw ourselves speaking in court, and to our horror, we became local celebrities for a while. Our faces were on the front page of the newspaper, clips of the DVD showed up on TV news shows, and we were recognized everywhere we went. A clip of Beth saying, "I have now lost both of my children," played in a loop on the news for days.

I went to a convenience store a day or two after the sentencing to get a few copies of a newspaper that was reporting our case. I paid for them, and when I walked back outside and got into my car, I saw the employees gathered in a group, staring at me out their window. I was thankful our notoriety passed quickly, mainly because we refused to do interviews.

We were hungry to become normal people once again—or at least semi-normal, since I was about to continue my work with Alberto so I could learn to become a shamanic healer.

Beth

I was in Josh's room, putting away his clothes, and I felt him behind me. When I turned around, he threw his arms around me, and we hugged.

"Where have you been?" I asked him.

He laughed and said, "I'm home." I though he meant our home in Waunakee, but later, I realized he meant heaven.

Then I saw Jessica, who told me they needed to go because they were late.

"What time do you need to be back?" I asked.

Jessica answered, "Time is different here. There is late, and then there's really late.

Josh added, "A month down there is like a day up here."

15

Two Out of Three

Beth

By February 2000, the sentencing was behind us. There were no more attorney phone calls or court appearances when we attended our first eight-day "Healing the Light Body" workshop with Alberto. It was a relief that we weren't on TV any longer and that Rick's family had stopped asking us for money. Rick and I could finally focus on ourselves, specifically on our healing, as we tried to make some sense of our lives since the kids were gone. It was a relief to know that one more dangerous drunk was off the streets and behind bars, where he couldn't hurt anyone else. That had been our worst fear. Finally, we didn't have to worry anymore because he had been sentenced.

Since the terrible day that changed our lives forever, Alberto had given me more hope and understanding than anyone else. When we'd met him for the first time in Salt Lake City at the Medicine Wheel gathering, he had suggested we learn more about his Light Body healing work, and Rick was anxious to jump in. He felt intensely drawn to healing work and shamanism. I was happy to go anywhere with Rick, and I looked forward to spending more time with Alberto and finding creative ways to embrace the spirit world where my children lived.

In Wisconsin, when we dared to mention anything about Spirit, it was as if we were speaking a different language from our friends and family. Most people there didn't understand it, or they didn't want to talk about it. It would be a relief to be with people who embraced the spirit world once again, who weren't afraid to try something new. And I was so hoping for more communication from my kids. I was relieved that I didn't have to hide my belly anymore (it was becoming impossible). Rick and I were on our way to spend a little over a week with Alberto on a retreat, doing sessions with him and learning more about Inka healing techniques. Communication with the kids was still my main focus when we flew to California and checked in at the retreat center, not far from Napa Valley.

Rick

Back in Wisconsin, Beth and I had met a man in the Madison area who had been a shaman. This was pretty soon after the accident, and he had asked Beth to lie down on the ground. When she did, he began to do what he called a "soul retrieval" to help her heal. I hadn't judged him or his methods. I was simply interested and hopeful, and I remembered that he had begun the healing with Beth and then stopped. "This isn't going to work," he said. "You two are so connected I have to do you both at the same time." He asked me to lie down next to Beth. I did, and he worked on us together.

This man had led a drumming circle after the healing, and people did what they called "journeying," where they used the drumbeats to enter an altered state and travel to a nonordinary reality or the spirit world. I went to a weekend seminar and joined the circle, but I struggled with the journeying part. I really didn't feel very much, and I wondered why. But with Alberto, my experiences were visceral. I felt the energy. I was enthusiastic and hopeful about the work, and I wondered what was in store for Beth and me during the coming eight days.

The retreat center was large and spread out, located on sacred Indian ground. There was a main cabin with a large meeting room that had exposed rafters, track lighting, and a kitchen where they prepared our meals. Down the road from the main meeting room were several log cabins with smaller meeting rooms and dorms that slept six or eight people. There were also smaller log cabins for two with a bathroom, a shower, and a huge fireplace. Rick and I stayed in one.

Main cabin in California

On that first day, we put our things away, and holding hands, Rick and I walked along the path that led to the main meeting hall. We had not done all of the requisite Medicine Wheel trainings that laid the foundation for the healing techniques we were about to learn. But since Alberto knew us from our time in Peru, he said that we were ready to go straight to the Light Body training. If there was anything we had missed that we needed to know, he promised to help us catch up.

When we gathered in the meeting room that evening, we didn't know any of the others besides Alberto and Lisa, one of his assistant teachers who had been with us in Peru. It didn't matter to me that we were with strangers because these were people who thought the way we did and who believed in the unseen realms, and like us, they all wanted to learn more and be able to heal themselves. I knew that Rick was also ready to learn about healing others. He seemed excited about the work. I, on other hand, still needed to heal myself so I focused on what I could learn to make my world acceptable.

A few days after we arrived, I had a dream in which Josh came to me. All I could see was a white screen, and then his beautiful green eyes appeared, and he said to me, "I'm proud of you, Mommy." I had asked both kids several days earlier if they were proud of me because getting through each day was so difficult, so his words meant a lot because I knew he had heard me.

Rick

Our sessions started at eight in the morning. We had several breaks to eat and relax throughout the day, and we finished at about eight or nine each evening. The surroundings were woodsy and beautiful, and I loved going for a run each morning before breakfast. But I kept my eyes open. Alberto had warned us about wild mountain lions, and I saw them a few times in the distance.

While I ran, I had time to think about what was happening to Beth and me. I noticed a lot of positive changes in Beth when we spent time with Alberto. We were both happy to leave town since we didn't have to deal with the courts and the attorneys anymore. And then, I was intrigued with something Alberto had said. I wasn't sure if he had said it in Salt Lake City or Peru. Maybe it was in both places. He told us that traditionally, a person was called to be a shaman in one of three ways:

1. You could heal yourself from a serious illness.
2. You could heal from a major tragedy.
3. You could get struck by lightning.

We were in California where it hardly rained, so I figured I wasn't about to get struck by lightning. That was more likely to occur in Wisconsin. And thank God I didn't have to heal myself from a serious illness. But both Beth and I had survived a major tragedy. It was one out of three, and I was hopeful that my work would keep deepening since Alberto told me that I had been a shaman in a past life. I believed what he said. I felt it in my bones, but what really mattered was that I was drawn to the work. I felt a true affinity with it, and Beth was getting a lot out of it, too. Beyond that, I would just wait and see.

Although we had been with Alberto before, we were newbies to the Light Body work, and we listened carefully to his lectures. The days were structured into sections in which we listened to the teachings, observed the exercises, and then broke apart into smaller groups to practice the healing techniques. Late one evening, early in the week, there were several of us working after class. Beth was sitting beside me, and when we had our hands over the person on the ground while we practiced sensing energy, suddenly I felt a tremendous rush of energy pouring into me. I instinctively pulled my hands back, and I couldn't move.

Beth

I was sitting beside Rick. Lisa was watching us as we were trying to sense the energy of the man who was lying on the ground. I looked outside the room for a moment. It was dusk, and I saw a flash of light in the sky. I figured it was lightning. We saw plenty of that in Wisconsin, but wait a minute—we were in California. It wasn't raining, and I thought that was really weird. I watched the flash of light enter the room and light up one of the walls. Suddenly I realized something was happening to Rick. The light seemed to hit his body. He remained kneeling, but he seemed stunned. His eyes were closed, and he was breathing deeply.

Lisa called out to Alberto. "Quick," she told him, "come over here. We need you."

"What's happening?" Alberto asked as he walked over to our group.

"Rick is having some difficulty," Lisa explained.

I looked outside again. There was no rain or thunder. We weren't having a storm, but I had seen the flash of light as plain as day. So had the other people in the room.

Alberto told Rick, "You have to get up and move your body. Right now. You have to move that energy through your body so it doesn't get stuck in your joints. I saw the lightning come into the room, but I didn't know where it landed," he added quietly.

Rick was kneeling, dumbstruck. I could see he was trying to move, but he didn't seem to be able to do it. I wasn't afraid, though. I knew Alberto would help him, but I was relieved when Rick finally struggled to get into a standing position. He was dripping with perspiration, and Alberto kept telling him to get up and move. "If you don't move," Alberto said, "that energy will cripple you."

In the meantime, the lights in the room began to flicker, one by one. The speed of the flickering increased until the lights began to look like strobes in a disco. It was as if Josh had jumped in and was playing with the electricity as he had done in the funeral parlor.

"Do your forms," Alberto told Rick. "Keep moving." He was referring to Rick's martial arts training that he had been doing for fifteen years. "Do your basic forms," Alberto repeated.

It seemed like Rick couldn't speak, but with his eyes closed and breathing very hard, he began to do the basic grounding moves that were the foundation of his martial arts training.

Rick

I heard Alberto telling me to get up and move, but I wasn't sure how to do that. I wanted to ask him, but I couldn't speak right then. Finally, I managed to stand up, and I slowly began to run through my martial arts forms. With each kick or punch or block I performed, I could feel waves of energy rolling off my arms and legs. I don't how long it was before Alberto told me to go outside, to take off my shoes, to put my feet directly on Mother Earth, and to continue doing my forms. I did as I was told, and eventually, I started to feel fluid and more like myself again. Alberto explained, "Spiritual lightning came into this building, and it hit you. It wanted you."

My body started to loosen up, and I eventually began to cool down as I knelt down with my hands and knees touching the ground. It felt like my body was being sucked into the earth, and I remained in that position for a little while. I wasn't sure what had happened, but when Beth and I walked down the path that night after the sessions toward our cabin, all my senses felt heightened. I was hyperaware. I could feel energy in the woods. I could sense animals around us, and I could hear things I didn't normally hear.

Once we were in our cabin, we lay down to sleep, but for me, sleep was out of the question. I was feeling so much coursing through me, I needed to do something. Beth had to turn away from me, so much energy and heat were coming off me. I got up and made a huge fire in the fireplace. I kept stoking the fire. It got bigger and bigger until Beth got up and asked me to stop. There was too much heat in the room, she told me, so I walked outside to breathe in the air. The sound of crickets was deafening. I could sense all the birds around me, and I could almost hear the plants talking to me. I felt in tune with everything that I could see and hear, and I knew that I would never be the same. I went back inside and tried to sleep. I think I dozed for two or three hours, but in the morning, I didn't feel tired at all.

At breakfast, people were buzzing about what had happened. Alberto hadn't talked to me about it, but the rumors were flying that something unusual had happened to me, that I had been struck by lightning, although there hadn't been any kind of a storm. When we headed into the large meeting room before the morning lecture, Alberto walked over and asked me how I felt. He wanted to make sure that nothing negative was going on, that I had no stiffness in my joints, and I assured him I felt fine. Alberto didn't come out and tell me exactly what had happened, but once the class began, he asked me to talk about my experience. As I tried to describe the heightening of my senses to the people around me, I knew for sure that I had been struck by spiritual lightning.

In case I was having any doubts, two nights later, it happened again when there were just a few of us practicing the healing techniques in the main meeting hall. It wasn't as dramatic; neither Beth nor Alberto was there, but I recognized the feeling when the energy began to course through me. I remembered what I was supposed to do. I needed to get up and move, but when I tried, the four or five people in the room were pushing me down. They were afraid for me to get up, but I managed to get up to a standing position, and I began doing my martial arts forms. It didn't last as long as the first time, but I was certain about my path at that point. I thought back to the three ways a person could become a shaman. Now I had been struck by lightning, *and* I had survived a major tragedy. I had experienced two out of three.

Beth

It's hard to admit this, but when Rick was struck by spiritual lightning, I was envious. During the rest of the week, we were getting an overview of shamanism and learning the Inka history and philosophy, and we were practicing techniques. We were building our mesas and infusing the stones with our healing experiences, and we were building sand mandalas. But when word got out about what had happened to Rick, everybody wanted him to heal them.

I was also up against a personal barrier that confused me. We were working on letting go of the past, but how could I let go of a past that I loved and desperately wanted back? I didn't want to do that. "I don't want to let go of my children," I told Alberto one day. "I know the work is to release the past, but I want to hold on to it."

I said this more than once, and I think the group was very patient with me, but I was pretty stuck, and I was resentful that Rick spent most of his free time working on people instead of being with me. I needed him, and he was preoccupied, so the rest of that week was pretty hard for me. I eventually realized that I didn't need to let go of my children. I just needed to release the trauma and energy that had taken so much of my vitality, but it took a while for me to understand that.

Once we were back home, Alberto was encouraging Rick to accelerate his shaman work, and he signed up for most of the workshops during March. I was too pregnant to accompany him. I tried to let him go, but when I looked at a calendar at the end of the month, I realized that he had been gone for twenty-two days that month. I had to say something. The birth of the baby was close, and I needed Rick by my side, so I asked him to stay home with me. He saw that I needed him, and I was relieved that he spent most of April by my side.

On May 12, close to my due date, I had an appointment in Madison with Dr. Karla Dickmeyer, my OB/GYN. That morning, she ruptured my membranes to get the labor started. By early evening, it was time, and Rick took me to the hospital. Karla was not on call, but at some point during my labor, she arrived and stood by my side. I was seven centimeters dilated. There were about six other babies being born that night, but Karla knew our history. "I'm going to put a live, healthy baby in your arms," she promised me. "I'm not leaving you."

The labor was excruciating. Karla's eyes were glued to the monitor, until she said, "I'm going to give you an epidural. You're still at seven centimeters, and the pain may be stopping the baby from coming out."

Rick

We trusted the doctor, and she gave Beth an epidural, but nothing changed. Beth's labor wasn't progressing, and in a split second, with her eyes glued to the monitor, the doctor determined that the baby was in distress. She sprang into action like a mother tiger with her claws out, rushing Beth into surgery. She performed a cesarean section on Beth, and at 2:30 a.m. on May 13, she lifted Gabriel Joshua out of Beth to find the umbilical cord wrapped around his neck. She had saved him, and she had saved us too.

On May 14, Sunday, Beth was receiving visitors, thrilled not only with Gabriel but also that it was Mother's Day. I stood there, happy and proud, and also amazed that since Jessie's birth, close to eleven years prior, Beth had always been a mother on Mother's Day. And now, despite the accident and all the suffering that went with it, this year was no exception.

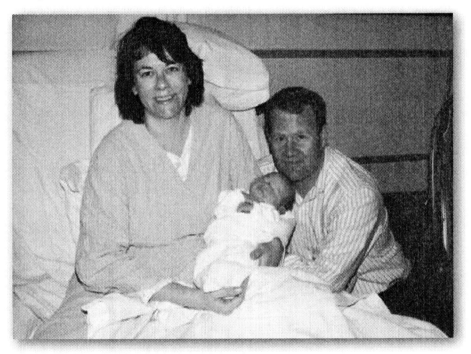

Gabriel Joshua on Mother's Day

16

Going Forward

Beth

$\mathcal{I}$T WAS JUNE 4, 2000, when I stood at the entrance to the Holy Angel's Church in West Bend with Gabriel Joshua in my arms. We had so much history here it was almost like seeing ghosts. My parents had gotten married in the sanctuary, the same place where we had walked down the aisle behind Jessica and Joshua in their casket. And now, I was about to baptize our son, who was a month old.

I wasn't taking any chances this time. Although I was certain that our children were with God, I had gone on a downward spiral around the fact that they had died without being baptized. As a result, I had decided to baptize Gabriel right away, just in case, and we had invited the same people who had been there for the funeral. About a hundred people had shown up, most of whom had grieved with us a year earlier. They had been with us in the worst of times. Now, we were all gathered at the best of times to celebrate Gabriel's birth. It was a time for joy.

I was not the same person I had been a year ago. That was for sure. But as joyful as other people were feeling, I was still deeply sad. It had been almost a year since I had kissed my children good-bye, and my relationship with God was on shaky ground. At least I was still here. I hadn't killed myself, and Rick and I were together, closer than we were before.

I had a lot to be happy about. And I held a blessing in my arms, a symbol of new life, a gift from God, and the promise of future happiness.

When I told a friend that God and I weren't on speaking terms, he'd said with a smile, "Do you really think God is worried that you're not talking to Him?"

Obviously not, since He had given me Gabriel. But I had yet to forgive Him. That would come a few years later.

We had asked my oldest brother, Steve, to be Gabe's godfather. We had wanted my sister Jeannie to be his godmother, but she couldn't be present at the baptism. My mother suggested we have Steve and his wife, Connie, as godparents, along with Jeannie and her husband, John. That felt right, and now Gabe has two sets of godparents to love and nurture him.

When I walked inside the church, I scanned the pews. They were filled with family and friends who had been with us before, during, and after the accident. I was so glad we could bring them happiness after they had endured such a hard time with Rick and me. We were offering them a form of healing as we showed them the changes that had taken place in us since the funeral. For some of our guests, this was the first time they had seen us for almost a year. We hadn't consciously planned this event as a healing experience for them, but when I looked at the joy and anticipation on their faces, I was gratified that we could give them a sense of closure—a little bit of happiness. Now that we were moving on, they could do the same.

When the ceremony was finished, we had a reception with a buffet in the basement of the church. We went from person to person, hugging each one and smiling. There had been a collective sense during the funeral that God was not there. Now, when they looked at Gabriel, it was clear that God was here. After all, I had a baby in my arms once again. Finally, our friends and family got to see, up close and personal, that we had a new baby, we were in a completely different place from last year, and we were a family again, and they were deeply relieved to see us happy and smiling.

Rick

The baptism was a great comfort to Beth. It was an important step for her, not necessarily back to Catholicism but rather back to her relationship with God. She wasn't all the way there, but I was glad to be with her and to bring a sense of closure to so many people who had been good to us all year long. It was gratifying to hug them and to see them smile, and I knew how much it meant to Beth.

As for me, in the spirit of shamanism, I decided to create a fire ceremony to commemorate the one-year anniversary of the accident. When Beth and I found out that the city was rebuilding the roads and the intersection where the accident had occurred, we went there and removed all the teddy bears, stuffed animals, flowers, and cards that people had so generously left in the kids' honor. There was a ton of stuff. We weren't sure what to do with it. I realized that a fire ceremony would be the perfect way to dispose of these items while honoring the people who had left them. We kept the crosses that I had made, but we took all the other items to our friends who had a farm and lots of empty space. That was where I would build a fire for the outdoor ceremony.

The Inkas view a fire ceremony as an offering. They believe that objects such as the ones left at the crash site contain prayers; burning them releases those prayers to heaven. My intent for this ceremony was to do just that, to transform what had happened, to release the prayers contained in the objects and send them to heaven. But whom would I invite?

There was no one in our immediate lives who knew anything about shamanism. It would be a stretch for everyone, so we decided to invite the people who were the most accepting of the changes we had made in our lives. We ended up extending an invitation to fifteen people who had also been at the baptism. Although none of them were familiar with fire ceremonies, they were all willing to show up for us, to let us be ourselves, and to learn. One of my friends said, "Rick, I really don't know what you're talking about and what you want to do, but I'm honored to be asked, and I'll be there." It was pretty much the same with everyone else.

It was one year to the day since the accident. The sun went down, and the full moon lit up the earth on July 18, 2000. At about nine o'clock, we gathered in a circle around a large fire I'd made on our friend Jean's land. Gabriel was asleep inside the house. Beth was at my side as I opened the sacred space by traditionally calling in the energies of the four directions: south, west, north, and east, as well as the earth below and the sky above. I explained to our guests that fire ceremonies predated what we knew about shamanism. While they were a definite part of shamanism, they began way back when human beings first gathered around the fire for warmth, protection, and companionship. A fire ceremony allowed bonds to be reinforced, and from a shamanic standpoint, it created sacred space to allow healing and ceremony to take place while it released the prayers to the heavens.

I handed a stick that I had gathered earlier to each of the ceremony participants, and we watched the flames soar and crackle until I felt a very strong spirit presence. I kept it to myself, but I knew there were a lot of spirits there. I could feel them, and I also knew that the kids were there because I get a certain physical sensation when they're around me. While the flames danced and leaped and created a lot of light, I guided everyone to silently put their prayers into the stick they were holding by blowing their intent into the stick with their breath. Then, one at a time, each person would go up to the fire, put in his or her stick, and see the prayers being released.

When that was finished, Beth and I began to put the objects from the crash site into the fire. I watched the energy release, rise up, circulate, dissipate, and rise up again. I said to our friends, "If you want to actually see the energy, watch the fire, unfocus your eyes, and you can see stuff moving around the fire."

We all watched the fire become huge, and it got so hot, we had to step back. Several people told me later that they had glimpsed the spirit energy momentarily and had felt uplifted. One of the participants, Chris, was a devout Catholic who had been our neighbor in Waunakee. He had been so kind to us when we were in the throes of our grief. "I saw things," he told me, "and I know what I saw." But he couldn't explain it. There was no place for that in his religion, and a few days later, he went to see his priest to talk and help him make sense out of what he had seen.

"What did he tell you?" I asked, thinking to myself that a priest maybe wasn't the best choice for a discussion on shamanism. But I was surprised when Chris said, "He told me there are things out there that we don't understand. He said there were all kinds of possibilities."

I was impressed with the priest's response. While he couldn't understand what Chris had seen and how it all worked, at least he was open.

When the crash site objects had completely disappeared and turned to ash, the fire continued to burn as Beth and I walked from person to person, hugging each of them individually and saying thank you. My intent for this ceremony had been twofold. First and foremost, I had wanted to honor our kids, and we had done that. Second, I had wanted to honor all the people who had given us their prayers and their sacred objects. We had done that too. It was about eleven o'clock when I said, "The ceremony is over. I just need to stay here and tend the fire."

People milled around. Some stayed for a little bit before eventually heading toward the house to get their things. When everyone had left, I stood alone by the fire, watching the flames flicker and the energy circulate, and I felt content inside. This had truly marked a passing for Beth and me. We had come a long way in a year. We had a long way to go, but we had become much stronger. We had embraced the spirit world where our kids lived, we had honored our friends, and we had begun to heal our hearts. Now we could devote our love to Gabriel, to each other, and to whatever came next.

I felt an affinity with the flames that seemed to move and soar as I watched. This was a good anniversary, and while we had some healing left to do, Beth and I were well on our way. We had figured out what made sense to us, we had embraced the spirit world, and we stood firm in who and what we had become. We were stating it to our closest friends. "This is who we are," we told them as we took a stand, "and this is what life is going to look like for us. Accept it, come with us, or it's been nice knowing you."

The fire had become embers when I sent out my final prayers for the evening. I told the kids good-bye, I thanked the spirits for being there, and I prayed to the four directions and the earth and the sky to close the sacred space. I took one more glance at the fire, which was still smoldering. I turned my back, and I walked toward the house to start my new life.

Epilogue

Beth

I T WAS SPRINGTIME in 2006 when Rick and I noticed that the trees we had planted all around our house were blooming. It seemed like everything was having a growth spurt, including me. I felt like I was waking up from a long, painful sleep that started when I was thirty-four, when we lost the kids. I had just turned forty-one when I looked in the mirror and asked Rick, "Where did my thirties go? What the heck happened?"

I felt like Rip van Winkle, finally waking up, as if I'd been doing life on autopilot. In a sense, it was true. I'd been going through the motions of my life, doing what I had to do while I was trying to heal from a kind of trauma that I am grateful most people never even have to imagine.

When our lawsuit, the civil side of the proceedings, settled in August 2000, it was one more painful reminder that our lives had been turned inside out. It was a year after the accident, and Fred was out of town, when we heard the doorbell ring. When we opened the door, there stood Rob and his wife, holding a bowl of raspberries from their garden, a gift for us. We invited them in and headed to the family room in the basement. It was the same room where we had met Jim Phillip a little over a year ago.

After Rob told us that they had just shipped their kids off to summer camp so they could have a quiet summer (what wouldn't I have given for some kids making noise?), he handed us the raspberries and a check made out to Rick and me. A third of our settlement was subtracted. Rob had shamelessly taken his cut even though there had been no trial, and he expected us to be OK about it. It wasn't about giving up the money; it was about the fact that I considered it unfair for anyone to profit from our terrible losses.

It was just one more travesty, one more loss that we had to endure, but we decided to move on and deal with something positive. I was still sad most of the time, and caring for an infant isn't easy in the best of times. Rick said to me, "I know that your dreams died with the kids that day. But now, I'm going to build you your dream house. I'm going to make your dreams into reality." Rick did what he promised. Our home has a big play area outside, a pool, geothermal heating, and lots of land where the kids can run and play. Today, we are a healthy, happy family of five. Let me introduce you to our beautiful children, our three gifts from God.

Gabriel Joshua, our oldest, was born on May 13, 2000. He is outspoken, social, and personable, equally comfortable being alone or playing with other kids. Gabe was exposed to shamanic traditions, both before he was born and during the first year of his life, so he has an affinity toward energies. He looks tough at first glance, but he's a very loving, caring guy, deeply affected when he thinks someone else is being hurt. In fact, he was so high-strung when he was an infant, we had to put a tent over the top of his crib so he wouldn't climb out when he was supposed to be taking a nap.

Athletics has become a big part of his life, but it was not at first. He can become very focused when he wants to, and that focus has paid off, not only in athletics but in several aspects of his life. He shies away from risk when he encounters something new, but in a short time, he jumps in with enthusiasm. He was born during the chaotic period after the accident when we lived in three different houses, so he had a lot of upheaval. But now he's very well adjusted. A good kid, he hates to disappoint us, he loves to make us happy, and he adores his brother and sister.

Benjamin James, our middle child, was born about sixteen months later, on October 4, 2001. Joshua had the middle name James, and so does Rick. Ben was a bit of a loner at first, but now he loves to hang out with his friends. He likes to be occupied and hides his feelings more than his brother does. He doesn't want people to know what he's feeling, but like his brother, he's also very sensitive.

Ben is naturally athletic. He has a great sense of humor, likes the family environment, and goes to great lengths to make us all laugh. He plays with his sister more than Gabe does, although these days, they're all getting along really well. Ben is almost as tall as Gabe, only one inch shorter, and he and Gabe have a good-natured competitive relationship. Still, Ben is the quiet one, and for some reason, maybe because he looks so much like Josh, after he was born, I didn't miss Joshua as much.

Grace Jessica, born on August 11, 2004, is the undisputed princess in the house. When she doesn't like something, she lets us know. She is soulful and caring, like Jessie was, loath to hurt or exclude anyone. Strong and athletic like her brothers, Grace plays volleyball. She studied gymnastics for two years, but when it was time to learn to do the splits, she opted out because she has a very low pain threshold. We're trying to explain to her that getting a paper cut and breaking a bone warrant different decibels of screaming. She's learning.

She and Ben are like two peas in a pod, but Gabe is a little more removed from Grace. Maybe he didn't like a princess taking over in the house, but they're getting more comfortable with each other. Grace is smart and pretty, and she did some department-store modeling a few years back. Now, she's learning to play the flute and the piano, and she likes cooking and other kinds of homebody activities. I thank God for all of them every single day.

In case you're wondering, God and I are back on speaking terms. I gave Him the silent treatment for about three years, but then I started praying, and God and I talked the whole thing out. I forgave Him, and I even managed to forgive David Raemisch, with the help of Gabe. I thought that forgiving that man would betray Jessie and Josh. But then one day, Gabe told me he was asking God to forgive Raemisch. I decided if my nine-year-old son could forgive him, I could too. I heard that he had become a pastor during his jail sentence, so I guess he made his own peace with God.

One day, I walked into the room in our new house we had designated for Jessie and Josh. We had put Jessie's dresser and bed in there, and we had placed their things on two high shelves along the walls of the room. I sat on the bed and told the kids I was truly happy in my life again. I knew they couldn't be happier for me. I hoped they wouldn't mind, but we packed up their items and moved Gabe into that room since he had been asking for his own room. In movies, you sometimes see rooms after a child has died and their parents have never changed anything. They're trying to hold on, but in truth, they're living in the past. It was important to Rick and me to let go of the past and not let our living children be affected by what happened to us before they were born. We were adamant about that ever since I got pregnant with Gabe. So when he needed his own room and his privacy, we wanted to honor that.

I still send kisses to Jessie and Josh each night before I go to sleep, and while I don't do the kind of shamanic journeying that Rick does, I have my own way of communicating with the kids. I do it in my dreams. As I have already explained, they are more than just dreams. They are like entering another world, the spirit world, where my kids live.

It all started with the chicken in the basket story. That was my first proof that the spirit world was accessible and that my kids could send me messages. When we decided to share the story with other people, I had no idea how far and wide it would go. It just seems that time and again, I get placed in close proximity to people who need to hear it.

It had only been about a year after the accident when Rick and I took a trip to Las Vegas for a business convention. We were staying at the MGM Grand Hotel, and Rick was wandering through the casino. I still had ahold of his shirttails so I was walking with him until we sat down at one of the blackjack tables so Rick could play a few hands. There was only one man seated at our table, and he was mindlessly playing with a chip. He and I struck up a conversation. I quickly found out that this was the one-year anniversary of his daughter's death. He needed to be in a place where there were lots of other people. I felt moved to tell him the chicken in the basket story, and no one else sat at our table until I finished it. I saw a look of relief on this man's face, and I was sure that Spirit had arranged this meeting.

Another example was in 2008, when Rick and I and our three kids were on our way to Disney World in Florida. Grace and I were sitting on the right side of the plane, and Rick and the boys were on the left. A woman walked over and said she was changing seats so a family could sit next to each other. She got into the window seat beside Grace and me, and I asked her if she was on vacation.

"No, I'm on a business trip," she said. I noticed that she kept twirling her necklace with her hands, and I asked her about it. She said she had lost her son a year ago. She was having a very hard time getting over it. He had been in a freak accident in the military. "I still have his ashes," she said. "I wear them around my neck, and I still set a place for him at the dinner table. My family, especially my husband, would like me to stop, but I can't let go. I want to keep remembering him."

I was sure that she needed to hear the chicken in the basket story, so I told it to her. Grace was quiet while this woman and I talked, mother to mother, about our losses, and we both cried. "Don't you think your son arranged for us to sit together?" I asked her. "Spirit is telling you he's OK, and it's OK to move on. You'll never forget him."

At one point, Rick looked over and saw us both crying, and he knew exactly what was going on. I took her phone number. Sometime later, I sent her a text message letting her know I was thinking about her and hoping she was doing well.

Things like this kept happening to me, at least five or six times. Rick and I had met with our writer in Los Angeles, and we were heading home. It was 2014. We had just spent a weekend working on our book when we arrived at Burbank Airport to start our journey home. We were sitting in the gate area, waiting to board the plane, when we heard an announcement. There was a problem with the toilet facilities on the plane, and the flight was being delayed.

We had a connection to make so when we asked the ticket agent what to do, she rerouted us to Los Angeles International Airport (LAX). We got into a taxi. It was a long ride. We checked in at LAX and waited for our flight. We had our boarding passes stamped, and we were standing in the Jetway when I noticed that I'd been given a window seat. I'm a little bit claustrophobic, and I prefer the aisle, so when I heard a woman behind me say she was unhappy with her aisle seat, we agreed to switch. It turned out that I sat in the middle with Rick on one side and this woman on the other. She and I started talking.

I asked her if she was on vacation, and she said, "No, it's kind of sad. I'm going to my cousin's funeral."

"That's why you're sitting next to me," I said.

"What do you mean?"

"This isn't the first time this has happened," I said, and I explained to her that we were writing a book about losing our children. You can guess what happened next. I told her the chicken in the basket story, and she promised to tell it to the children of her cousin who had died.

The same kind of thing happened when I went to get an oil change for my car a month later. I began talking to a salesman and found out he had a friend who had lost a three-year-old child in a hit-and-run accident. I told him the story, and he asked permission to share it. Of course, I gave it to him.

When we first heard the story so many years ago, after we had shared it with our families, we got an inkling that one day we would write our own book. But we had no idea the major role that this story would play. Now that our book is complete, we feel that the chicken in the basket story is the turning point, and we would like to offer it here as a symbol of hope. Time and again, it's been clear that God wants me to share the story with other people who are undergoing the worst possible losses. I want to show them that we not only survived, but we also found richness, meaning, and purpose in our lives once again. I believe that Jess and Josh in spirit want that for us, and I believe that other people's loved ones want the same for them.

I never did receive a text from God, but look at what He sent me instead!

Rick

It's been fifteen years since the kids are gone, and we have been on a long journey to heal ourselves. When I discovered shamanism and studied with Alberto, I learned that shamans are often referred to as great storytellers because they help people with the stories of their lives. Through the work that I did to heal myself and others, I have come to understand and appreciate the wisdom of the four directions:

> In the South, you shed your past, your old self, and look to perceive beauty.
> In the West, you step beyond death and fear.
> In the North, you step into your own journey and dream the world into being.
> In the East, you become one with Spirit.

It's been a long journey to heal ourselves, one that still continues, but Beth and I refused to give up on life or on each other. We refused to stop until we found a way, not only to get through our pain, but also to directly communicate with our children. Our particular ways may not be right for anyone else because everyone has different needs, but at least we can encourage others to stay open to their own possibilities and believe that they can be healed, no matter how bad it gets.

Beth and I made a pact before Gabe was born that we would not burden our new children with suffering or sadness or put pressure on them in any way. We teach them about safety, but we don't go overboard. We believe that the accident happened for a reason, so we have no reason to think this kind of thing will happen again. We already went through it once, and now, we feel like we are good to go.

When I look back, I see that building a new house with no memories played a large part in our healing. In 2001, we bought forty acres of farmland in Glenbeulah, Wisconsin, where we built a wonderful house and planted about a hundred and fifty trees over the course of seven years. The trees struggled like we did for a few years, but the time came when new growth sprang up and everything looked vibrant and alive. A new cycle was beginning; everything was waking up. Today, we're playing the normal (somewhat) family. I spend a lot of time with my kids, and although I'm not doing shamanic healings on a day-to-day basis, it's a part of me. For me, being a shaman feels like I signed a two-way pact. Spirit helped heal Beth and me and is willing to help when I call upon it. So I need to be open and available when it calls on me to help others. Spirit has put both of us in many different situations where we have been able to help others. Being able to write this book is one of them.

Since the accident, Beth and I have changed a lot. We have integrated the tangible world and the spirit world, and we can move between the two. I have always had a strong sense of acceptance that the accident was meant to happen. I can't say that Beth always agrees with me, but I feel certain that there was nothing we could have done to change it. I know I was supposed to be on this path, that Spirit has a master plan, and we are here, living it. And I can feel the kids around me a lot. They come to visit during meals, when we're in nature, when I'm falling asleep, and other times when I least expect it. When I sense the kids, I always tell Beth, and when she goes into the spirit world in her sleep and talks to them, she always tells me. In this way, we have become closer than we already were.

Sadly, many couples separate when they encounter the depth of tragedy that we did. Beth and I are still together after twenty-eight years of marriage because we never blamed each other. We refused to go that route, and we discovered that there is life after death. We each have found our individual ways to communicate with our kids, and I want readers to know that if you stay open and responsive, Spirit will work on your behalf.

It's all about looking at life from a different frame of reference than what we can see and touch. There is more than heaven and hell, and we are more than our physical bodies. We are energy. We can heal from the inside out, and when we change our frame of reference, we can live in two worlds at the same time. I look forward to a time in the distant future when our time is up here on earth and once again, we will all be together as a family.

In the first few months following the accident, I wrote a poem to Jessica and Joshua. We had it etched into their tombstone, and I'd like to share it with you now:

Your little souls were sent to us for a short time,
They left so suddenly, it seems for no reason or rhyme.
Your beaming faces, the sparkle in your eyes,
Is replaced by the tears we'll forever cry.
The laughter in your voice, the love in your heart,
How we long for these to fill the hole, now that we are apart.
We taught you many things, you enjoyed life so much
Now it is your turn to teach us, so that others we may touch.

Love,
Mom and Dad

Olsen family 2015

Acknowledgments

WE WISH TO thank the following people, who helped to make this book and our journey possible. Without them, the book and our lives would be much different: Andrea Cagan, for her love and support, as well as her amazing ability to take the pain, anguish, and hope that we spoke to her about and have it come alive on these pages; Pamela Kawi for the cover concept; Beth's parents for moving back when she asked them and for giving our children the love that only grandparents can give; and all of our friends, both old and new, who have given us their never-ending love and support.

Beth
Thank you to the four spiritual men in my life, without whom my journey would not have been possible: my husband, Rick; Jim Phillip; Alberto Villoldo; and Dan Francis.

Rick
Thank you to my wife, Beth, and my brother, Jeff, and his family.